A Field Guide in Colour to
DOGS

A Field Guide in Colour to
DOGS

By J. Novotný and J. Najman

Photographs by Z. Humpál

Text by Josef Novotný and Josef Najman
116 colour photographs and 124 b/w photographs by Zdeněk Humpál
1 colour and 2 b/w photographs by S. A. Thompson
1 colour photograph by Spectrum Colour Library
Pen drawings by Hana Strnadtová

Translated by Ruth Shepherd
Graphic design by Václav Kučera

English version first published 1977 by
Octopus Books Limited
59 Grosvenor Street, London W1

ISBN 0 7064 0611 7

Printed in Czechoslovakia
3/07/05/51-01

Contents

The Evolution of the Dog

Until recently several theories were current as to the origin of the dog. Some experts maintained that the ancestor of today's terrier, poodle and dachshund was a now extinct wild dog, others held the opinion that the dog was descended from the jackal and still others that the wolf must be acknowledged as the ancestor of the dog of today.

As long as there was insufficient comparative material to draw upon it was impossible to provide a more definite answer. But with the passage of time, skeletons of dogs were dug up on archaeological sites which threw more and more light on the origin of the dog.

The earliest finds of bones of the domestic dog date from the New Stone Age, the Neolithic period. They differ strikingly from the bones of the wolf and, in addition, they provide evidence of differences within the species of domestic dog. In fact it can be estimated that, even at that time, several types of dog were in existence.

The earliest known extinct dog was **Canis poutiatini.** It came from the European part of Russia and from Denmark and lived some 10 to 12 thousand years ago. However, we are not sure whether it was an already domesticated dog or a semi-wild animal held in captivity.

Another was the lake settlement dog, **Canis familiaris palustris,** which was already a domestic animal. It lived with human beings in their pile-supported buildings on the banks of rivers and lakes. This dog was similar in appearance and size to the spitz and could well have been the forefather of breeds such as the spitz, pinscher and the terrier. It lived during the New Stone Age and its bones were first discovered in Switzerland.

Also probably dating from the Early Neolithic period was **Canis familiaris leineri,** regarded as the ancestor of the greyhound.

Canis familiaris inostranzewi, whose original habitat was Russia, was much larger than the lake settlement dog and is thought to have been the forefather of the Great Dane and northern and herding dogs. Some believe that it was the outcome of crossing the lake settlement dog with the wolf.

Canis familiaris matris-optimae is reminiscent of the Alsatian or German Shepherd and is thought to be the distant ancestor of all European breeds of sheepdog. The scavenger, **Canis familiaris intermedius,** is recognized as the predecessor of all pointers, retrievers and spaniels, that is to say hunting dogs and poodles. Both of these date from the Bronze Age.

However, the opinion prevails today that the real ancestor of the dog is, after all, the wolf. This view is backed above all by the genetic affinities between the dog and the wolf for they both have the same number of chromosomes.

It is not long since the view that the dog was the earliest animal to be domesticated had to be abandoned. For it has been proved that even before the dog, goats, sheep, pigs, cattle and pigeons were domesticated.

But the fact remains that the dog came closest to the man and became his faithful friend, helper and protector and that a sociologically interesting relationship grew up between man and dog which has no counterpart as far as other domestic animals are concerned.

From time immemorial man has made use of particular aspects of the dog's physique and disposition to produce different breeds. Although this for long lacked any genetic basis — those types were promoted which were best suited to man's needs. Some of these have been bred for centuries to this very day with only minor changes; others became extinct and were replaced by breeds better suited to the changed conditions.

It was not until the middle of the nineteenth century, following the discovery of the laws of heredity, that the deliberate and purposeful breeding of dogs in the purebred form in which we know them today came about. Individual breeds are not crossed with each other and therefore their breed is pure-blooded. This means that the progeny of purebred parents are themselves purebred, having all the external characteristics and behavioural patterns of their breed.

This fact is of immense importance for dog breeders for it enables anyone to choose the breed whose appearance and disposition is most to his or her liking.

Up to the middle of the nineteenth century dogs were not bred witl. a clear end in mind. It is true that there were a number of breeds intended for specific purposes, particularly for various types of hunting, but dogs of these breeds were often crossed among themselves and no actual records were kept. So purebred dogs in the sense we know them today were non-existent.

Nevertheless certain breeds did maintain a characteristic type, so that it is possible to form a reliable picture of how some of the present breeds originated and to follow their family tree — at least in rough outline — quite a long way back.

Even today in some isolated regions, such as islands or mountain valleys, certain types of dog are found which belong exclusively to these localities and can be seen nowhere else. For whole generations the dogs in such areas could not be crossed with any other type so that some were perfected until they were virtually purebred.

Another environment where types of dog acquired a degree of stability at an early date were the courts of the nobility. In the kennels of noble families care was taken to mate only dogs with similar appearance and characteristics and to ensure that the best specimens left the most progeny. It was from these regionally differentiated types that many of the national breeds of today originated.

The origin of purebred dogs in today's sense of the word dates from the second half of the nineteenth century. At this time the practice of keeping records of the ancestry of individual dogs was begun; various dog-breeding societies were established which kept these records and issued pedigrees on the basis of them. In this period, too, the first standards or exact descriptions of various breeds were issued and the first dog shows were held.

Individual breeds differed from each other, not only as regards colour, the type of the coat and physical structure, but also in size and weight.

The great majority of breeds originated as hunting dogs. Different types of dog were needed for the various phases of hunting and for varying conditions. On the vast steppes of Russia, for example, there developed a dog, called the Borzoi, which was fast enough to catch any creature native to the steppes from the hare to the wolf. Dogs which go to earth owe their origin mainly to the need for an animal to bolt a fox from the lair when it has taken refuge from pursuing hounds. Breeds of gundogs showed hunters where game was hidden so that it could be caught in nets or — after the development of firearms— how to approach it for shooting.

Apart from its services in hunting, from the very beginning of its co-existence with man, the dog had another function — that of guard dog. For long generations some dogs came into contact only with their masters and their families and so were highly suspicious of strangers. They were encouraged to be wary and from that it was only a step to the deliberate breeding of dogs that were watchful and suspicious of strangers, in fact to the breeding of the service dogs of today.

Man and his Dog

At an early stage of their contact, man learned to recognize the good qualities of the dog and to use them for his own purposes. To begin with these uses were limited, but with the development of civilization, dogs were used for an increasing variety of human activities. Whenever a man needed a dog for a specific purpose, he tried to obtain a puppy from parents which had proved particularly apt in this sphere. So breeds came into being distinguished not only by their different external features but also by the most varied behavioural qualities.

In general, the origin of the breeds known today can be sought:

1. in isolated areas where an almost purebred type of dog developed, characteristic of the particular area;

2. at the kennels of the nobility where comparatively purebred features were maintained;

3. in the deliberate and purposeful crossing of various breeds with the intention of establishing a new breed with certain external and behavioural characteristics.

Whether a breed expanded or not was conditioned, in the first place, by its usefulness. and only in isolated cases by the fact that it was exceptionally interesting. There are some people who will always endeavour to obtain a breed which hardly anyone else has. If successful, other people usually begin to take an interest and a new breed comes into being. This pioneering work is not always successful. Either there is no particular use for the breed or it is unsuited to the climatic conditions of the country of its origin, or it does not arouse sufficient enthusiasm to ensure its continued expansion.

In enlarging breeds an important part is often played by the fashionable popularity of one breed or another. A wave of popularity may rise very quickly and then, after a few years, fade away and another breed comes to the fore. While such heightened enthusiasm does much for the expansion of the breeds, it is not always to the advantage of the type of dog concerned. For instance a boom can lead to a breed deteriorating because there are too few good stud dogs and brood bitches, unless sufficiently strict measures are taken by breeders' clubs to see that untypical individuals are not bred.

There are many examples which go to prove that, after sudden bursts of popularity only those breeds whose health and temperament have not suffered in the expansion maintain the desired level.

At the present time the popularity of large breeds is declining slightly and interest in medium-sized and small breeds is growing. A small dog does not need so much space, it is easier to take by car out of the town or city, and finally it does not need so much food. This, of course, does not mean that there is any real threat to the larger breeds but merely that there are fewer of them in towns and their breeding and keeping has transferred to the country. Large, long-legged dogs will have an assured existence as long as they are needed for work that a smaller dog could not perform.

What is clear, is that in the past breeds whose working function ended because of technological advances tended to become extinct. Some types of droving dogs for example disappeared when the need to move cattle on the hoof ended with the development of road and rail transport. Nowadays it is more likely that such breeds would survive, kept alive by the interest of dog show exhibitors and the pet-owning public.

The system of the breeding of dogs is based on the relationship of various breeds to each other as well as on their various uses and specific purposes.

The division of dogs according to their purpose has been stabilized into the following categories: **working, hunting, terriers, greyhounds, utility** and **toy** breeds.

Working dog is a term used loosely to describe a large group of dogs which provide various services for man, as for example, sheepdogs and other herding dogs, dogs used for haulage, police dogs, guide dogs, service dogs, guard dogs and so on. For the most part these are large dogs, highly intelligent, quiet, inherently wary and faithful.

Originally hunting dogs were also classed as working dogs once they had passed trials of efficiency as gundogs. Later, however, the term working dog was only applied to non-hunting breeds.

The next large group consists of dogs used mainly for hunting which led to the breeding and protection of game for sport. Their common feature is an exceptionally highly developed instinct for hunting which man, by means of training, has chanelled to meet his own needs.

Terriers were bred for centuries in the British Isles as hunting dogs and were used for bolting foxes and badgers in the same way as dachshunds were used on the European continent. Although with the passage of time many of them were weaned away from their original job, they retained some of their characteristic features, such as their temperament and instinct to hunt rodents even when they became house dogs. The Airedale Terrier which is also a member of this group has been successfully trained as a service dog.

Another special group is constituted by greyhounds. They too used to be classed as hunting dogs. Unlike other breeds of hunting dog, the greyhound is a sight hound using its eyes rather than its sense of smell.

In the last group are dogs of various breeds which do not usually perform any specific service for man other than that of being his companion — and as such are as important to him as the others though in different ways. A great many unrelated breeds fall into this group — dogs of different body structure, different size and with different types of coat and different colour. But whether they are large or small, black or white, short- or long-haired, they are characterized, above all, by their faithfulness and devotion to man. They are loyal companions to all who love animals and want their affection returned. But the utility dog fulfils its mission in other ways, too. In family life, it helps to form the character of children, teaches them love for living creatures, influences their behaviour and helps them to be unselfish. All these qualities contribute to the dog's value and fully justify its place at man's side.

Things to Remember when Buying a Dog

As we have already said, a dog is not merely a domestic animal, but also a friend. You must choose your dog just as you choose a friend or companion, not for a short time or for momentary amusement but to live with until fate parts you in a style which suits your individual characteristics, inclinations and tastes. In the vast kingdom of dogs everyone can find the very dog he wants if he approaches the choice of a breed seriously and responsibly.

First clarify in your own mind exactly what purpose the dog is to serve. If you need a working dog or a gundog, there will not be too many problems because the very reason for which you require the dog determines fairly accurately the most suitable breed. If, for instance, you want a sporting dog as a gundog for large shoots where mainly small furred and feathered game is shot, you will probably decide on some kind of pointer which can both point and retrieve. Your choice will be similarly simplified if you need a dog for any other particular task.

It is much more difficult for those who only know that they want a dog which will be their devoted companion. Many are badly informed, or have only minimal knowledge of the dog world, so that the breadth of choice simply baffles them. All too often their choice does not fall on the breed best suited for them and this can engender bitter disappointment.

A few lines should be devoted to helping those who are faced with the problem of choosing a dog which will fulfil their expectations. In the first place one should carefully consider all the consequences of bringing a dog into the household.

People of a nervous, highly strung disposition or who have nervous neighbours should not pick a noisy dog which likes to bark. It is true that patient training can transform such a holy terror into a pleasant companion but this entails a lot of work. It is much simpler and surer to pick a breed at the beginning that is not given to such a noisy self-expression.

In choosing a dog you should bear in mind your own character as well as your surroundings so that its nature and behaviour will fit in.

It should also be remembered that a dog must have exercise and that one must be prepared to take it out for a walk as frequently as it needs. Large, long-legged dogs or smaller very active ones naturally need more exercise than a quiet dog which often likes the comfort of the fireside better than long walks. If you have difficulty in walking then you should choose a dog which does not demand a great deal of exercise.

In addition to sufficient exercise, both on and off the lead, every dog needs to be kept busy. Some need serious work, as in the case of sheepdogs or gundogs; for others play is enough. You should therefore take into consideration what you can offer the dog, whether you will have enough time, opportunity and knowledge to give it sufficient training in its particular branch and whether you will be able to make use of the qualities with which nature has endowed it and which have been fostered in it for generations.

If you do not give the dog sufficient opportunity to enjoy life in its own way, it usually pines, its temperament finding outlets in the wrong direction so that either it becomes a bad dog or at best a disagreeable one.

Every dog also requires a certain amount of care. Wire-haired and long-haired varieties need more attention than short-haired, and those which have to be modelled into shape — such as the poodle — demand special care. Dogs should be brushed and combed every day — in the case of long-haired dogs brushing suffices — and twice a year they need a bath. Too frequent bathing is harmful. A dog can easily catch cold and becomes less resistant to infection. In addition its coat suffers, losing its natural oil and thus becoming dry and brittle. The water should be at a temperature of about 35° C and should reach only to the dog's abdomen. A mild soap or shampoo should be used and care should be taken that it does not get into the ears (which should be protected with tampons of cotton wool) or into the eyes. The head should not be bathed and should remain dry. After bathing, the dog should be well rinsed in lukewarm water and well dried. It should remain for at least two or three hours in a warm place until it is completely dry.

A dog should not be bathed in winter and a bitch in season or a pregnant bitch should not be bathed at all, nor should a puppy under one year old. However, if a young dog does get really dirty there is nothing for it but soap and water for the dirt must be removed, sometimes even from the head. Usually it is enough to rub the 'affected' spot with a sponge and tepid soapy water, in other cases more drastic measures are required, but great care should be used.

Dogs can be bathed out-of-doors, but only in summer in exceptionally warm weather. The dog should be allowed to shake itself well, then it should be rubbed down till it is dry and made to have a good run. In fine, warm weather, a dog can go into the water whenever it wants. The natural oil in the coat prevents the water from reaching the skin and so the dog does not catch cold.

Dogs with beards and moustaches should have their whiskers washed with warm water after meals. The inside of the ears should also be cleaned and so should discharges at the corners of the eyes. The cleaning of the ears should be restricted to the visible parts and it should be done with cotton wool, moistened with boracic solution or one-per cent salicylic acid and wound round an orange stick. Care should also be taken of the nails, especially if a dog does not have sufficient exercise to wear them down. The feet should be kept free of dirt, earth, small stones, thorns or other sharp objects which can get between the pads and the toes.

It quite often happens that a dog is ill. There are a number of diseases to which it is subject and diagnosis and treatment should be under the guidance of a veterinary surgeon. Dogs are all too often attacked by fleas, lice, nits, ticks and different tape, hook and round worms, and can suffer from ailments of the eyes and ears (especially if they travel in cars with open windows). They can also suffer from a chill of the bladder, constipation or diarrhoea, flatulence, kidney diseases, skin complaints, poisoning, paralysis of the hind legs (sometimes known as dachshund's paralysis), distemper and many other diseases.

Your can tell when a dog is ill by its depression, irritability and unaccustomed restlessness, tendency to crawl into a corner, whining, obvious tiredness, lack of appetite and increased temperature. The first signs of distemper are usually a mucoid or purulent discharge from the nose and eyes, septic blisters on the flanks, excessive thirst, lack of appetite and fatigue.

When a dog joins the family circle extra care must, of course, be taken with regard to hygiene. A dog should never be allowed to express its affection by licking one's face. Even the cleanest of dogs — and there are some which will go to any length to avoid every puddle — brings some dirt and even germs into the house. It should be given its own place in the house or flat where it will not be in anyone's way and should have its own sleeping quarters which should be kept scrupulously clean. Small dogs can have a smaller wicker kennel, medium-sized dogs a wicker basket and large dogs a mattress or several layers of rugs. The bed should be large enough for the dog to lie in it comfortably and, in the case of a basket, the entire bottom should be covered with a small mattress. This should be filled with coarse material — never feathers — and it should have a loose cover which can be removed for washing. If it is not possible to keep the dog indoors, it should have a sufficiently large fenced-in run in the garden or yard with a well-built kennel. This should have its walls insulated against damp and should not stand directly on the ground or be accessible to wind and rain.

The most important factor in the care of a dog is correct feeding. The quality and quantity of its food and regular feeding are decisive for the health of the dog and for maintaining its fitness.

The quantity depends on the calorific value of the food and on the size and age of the dog. Food should be varied and contain sufficient basic nutrients in the correct proportions to provide various kinds of energy and should, in addition, include vitamins, salts and trace elements.

About two-thirds of a dog's food should consist of meat. The dog is carnivorous and therefore meat and other animal products such as eggs, milk, cheese, should constitute the principal component of its food. Raw meat is most valuable but a dog fed exclusively on raw meat tends to be smelly. Offal and fish are also of considerable value. The best bones are veal bones which a dog can grind up. Quite unsuitable are long hollow bones or the bones of rabbits, game and poultry which can easily splinter and stick in the gullet.

Vegetable products are of less value but should be included in a dog's diet for their calorific value and vitaminal content. Most important are root vegetables, brown bread, barley, semolina, groats, pulse and other vegetables and fruit. Modern pet foods include excellent canned meats and a range of complete diets in pellet form. The latter provide satisfactory, if monotonous, nutrition and require little effort on the part of the owner.

Regular feeding is of great importance and a dog should therefore be fed at the same time each day. It should only be given as much food as it will consume immediately but fresh water should be available at all times.

Puppies should at first be fed four times a day, then three times and an adult dog not more than twice a day. After meals a dog should be allowed to rest for at least two hours.

A bitch in oestrus requires greater care. When she is in season she leaves stains behind her, at first brownish, then pale pink and afterwards colourless. The marks she leaves are always a problem whether she is kept indoors or in a kennel. If she has her bed in the house, the covers on her mattress should be frequently changed and her bedding and the whole flat or house thoroughly aired. She should be taken out early in the morning and late in the evening when there are not so many dogs about. If she is kept out of doors in a kennel, the straw should be changed frequently. And the doors and gates of the house, garden or yard should be kept closed all the time.

Bitches come in season twice a year, usually in spring and autumn. The first signs of her heat are that she is restless and urinates little and often.

If a bitch is to be mated, a note should be made of the date on which the first drops of blood appear. On about the 12th or 13th day bitches are usually ready to accept a dog, and easily allow themselves to be mounted. It is customary to take the bitch to the dog and not the other way round. If it is not yet the right time, the bitch may bite the dog.

A bitch in whelp should be given plenty of gentle exercise in the fresh air and sun but she should not be allowed to carry anything heavy or to jump. Pregnancy usually lasts from 59 to 63 days.

The bitch's feeding should be adapted to her condition. The diet can be enriched by the addition of liver, veal bones, raw eggs, fresh fruit and vegetables. Care should be taken that she does not become too fat.

The arrival of puppies creates a lot of work. To begin with the bitch takes complete care of them, nurses and massages them and removes all traces of their faeces. But once they begin to leave their box and crawl or run about the room there is nothing for it but to follow them round patiently clearing up the puddles and faeces after them. This has to go on until they are house-trained and it demands a great deal of time and patience.

As the puppies become independent, much time must be spent in preparing their food, putting them out regularly and beginning their basic obedience training.

A few weeks after their birth, the puppies should be given additional food. For the first two or three days they should be given scalded cow's milk, sweetened with a lump of sugar from twice to four times a day and then a thin gruel of semolina or other cereal. After a few days they can be given thicker porridge with more and more rolled oats being added. Porridge should be alternated with semolina and rice pudding.

In two or three weeks, the puppies' diet should be enriched by meat stock — once a day — and at five weeks old they can be given scraped or minced meat and lightly boiled eggs four or five times a day.

Once weaned — usually at five to six weeks old — puppies are entirely dependent on the food you prepare for them. It should be nourishing but easily digestible and should be given to them four times a day — always at the same time. It should consist mainly of minced lean beef — cooked or raw — eggs, minced liver, brown bread, sieved vegetables and fish oil. Raw meat must be absolutely fresh.

Great care should be devoted to hygiene. Make sure that the bitch has no fleas. Puppies infested by fleas become weak, their growth is stunted and they become less resistant to infections.

You should get rid of fleas with a safe insect powder which can be obtained from a chemist. The instructions must be followed exactly. The same means can be used to keep dogs free of lice and nits.

Here mention should be made of other parasites from which dogs often suffer. External ones include ticks, ear mites and lice; internal ones include tape, hook and round worms. Dogs with canker should be treated by a veterinary surgeon, whereas ticks can be dealt with by the owner. They should be removed in the same way as they are from human beings.

Dogs with tape worms suffer loss of appetite; they become thin and their coats lose their gloss. From time to time they vomit and suffer from diarrhoea followed immediately by constipation. The presence of tape worms can also be recognized by the way the dogs toboggan along the ground on their behinds. If any such signs are visible, consult your vet.

Some tape worms can be transmitted to human beings, so you should always wash your hands after stroking a dog. Besides this, care should be taken to prevent it from licking people even if it is healthy. Dogs should never be given plates or dishes from the table to lick.

Small puppies often suffer from round worms and dogs of six months and over from hookworms. The first are more dangerous because they are parasites on an undeveloped organism. Signs are similar to those in the case of tape worms and help should be sought from a veterinary surgeon.

It is not always easy to see that a dog has parasites so it is a good thing to take a specimen of the dog's stool to a vet twice a year for testing.

Naturally you want your dog to be well-behaved. Even if you have a small lap dog it should receive basic training. A badly behaved dog is always a bad companion.

Training should start the very day a new puppy is brought home and should continue unceasingly as part of an uninterrupted educational process. You only have to relax once and the dog will take advantage and refuse to obey. Sometimes it is hard to see that a dog is playing up and is trying in various ways to undermine your authority.

A young dog must at once be house-trained. It must be forbidden to creep into places that do not belong to it and must not be allowed to jump up at people even if it is looking forward to a treat such as a walk. A dog should also be trained not to take food from strangers, to come when it is called, to sit or lie down when told to, not to run away or to chase noisily after every car, motorcycle or bicycle and to walk to heel. In fact, even the smallest house dog should be well behaved and remember its manners even when it is not under the direct control of a member of the family.

Such training demands a great deal of work and patience, love and the correct approach to the dog as an individual, for even dogs of the same breed often have individual quirks. It is important to approach training in a well-considered, purposeful manner, calmly and consistently. You must not forget that much of what you are asking of the dog runs counter to its nature and that it will try to avoid cooperating whenever you give it the chance.

In educating and training the dog you must first make sure that it understands what you want. Its behaviour is instinctive and not the result of thought, so you should try to see that — right from the beginning — it grasps that there is a direct connection between what it does and the consequences which will be pleasant or unpleasant, in that either the dog will be praised by its master or it will receive a reprimand or a slightly painful punishment.

It is essential that the dog should not lose its confidence in you and that it should not be afraid of you. Every feeling of pain should come of itself and not be directly connected with you. So rather than beat or hit a dog you should throw a small pebble or some other small object at it, if it does something it is forbidden to do.

Praise must be loving, scolding sharp, commands short and always expressed in the same words and in the same sequence. The gestures which accompany the commands must always be the same, too. You must be patient and repeat every exercise until the dog understands exactly what you expect and learns to carry it out perfectly.

Education and training must arise from your love of the dog and its relationship to you, its devotion to you and its respect for the pack leader whom you replace. It is wrong to be nervous, get angry with the dog, shout at it or beat it, for this breaks down mutual harmony. Be careful not to spoil the dog because of your own lack of experience or failure to understand completely its 'logic'.

Finally, two pieces of advice: buy only a purebred dog and not one of uncertain origin and, if possible, provided you have the time and loving patience buy a puppy rather than an older dog.

By purebred dogs we mean those which come from purebred stock and whose pedigree proves them to be members of a certain breed. The pedigree contains extracts from the stud book and includes the names of the dog's ancestors usually as far back as its great grandparents. Choose a young dog in preference to an older one because it will give you its very first love which is always stronger than attachments formed later.

Before actually buying a dog you should of course realize that its arrival will bring anxieties and expense as well as joy.

How Dogs are Judged

Kennel clubs in individual countries, Great Britain included, and the FCI (Fédération Cynologique Internationale) to which breeders' organizations in 24 countries in Europe, Africa and Latin America belong and with which the United Kingdom and some other non-member countries have reciprocal agreements, issue standards for individual breeds of dog. These are descriptions of the general appearance of the dog and various components of the body. At dog shows it is the task of judges to estimate how closely the dog exhibited conforms to the standard, that is how nearly it approaches the ideal for the breed in question.

At shows in all countries, fairly uniform terminology is used for describing the general appearance of the dog, the structure of the body and other features so that the conformity of the dog to the standard can be estimated.

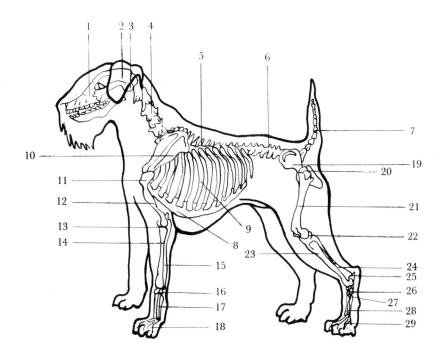

Fig. 1 **Skeletal Anatomy**:
1 facial part of the skull, 2 occiput, 3 atlas, 4 cervical vertebrae, 5 thoracic vertebrae, 6 lumbar vertebrae, 7 tail vertebrae, 8 breast bone, 9 ribs, 10 shoulder blade (scapula), 11 shoulder joint, 12 humerus, 13 elbow joint, 14 radius, 15 ulna, 16 wrist (carpus), 17 pastern (metacarpus), 18 toes, 19 pelvis, 20 hip joint, 21 thigh bone (femur), 22 knee joint, 23 shin bone (tibia), 24 fibula, 25 tarsus, 26 metatarsus, 27 instep joint, 28 instep, 29 toes

Terminology used in describing the general appearance of the dog

Body structure can be symmetrical, asymmetrical, well balanced, low, moderately low build, taller build. The dog can be too tall (that is to say compared with the standard), or too low. The balance of various parts of the body is also described: the dog can be long-legged, short-legged or the hind quarters may be higher than the forequarters.

Proportions — the ratio of the height at the shoulder to the length of the body. The dog can be square, oblong, small, large, short, long or conforming to the standard.

Type — the extent to which the dog, at first sight, approaches the ideal for the breed, that is, whether it is typical or not. Type also expresses the difference between dogs and bitches which should be clearly distinguishable — for a dog to resemble a bitch or a bitch to look like a dog is a fault.

Build — the state of development of bone and muscle structure which can be strong, weak, firm, coarse or fine. A dog is then commensurately massive, strong, weak, robust. If it gives the impression of clumsiness it is heavy, if the reverse it is light.

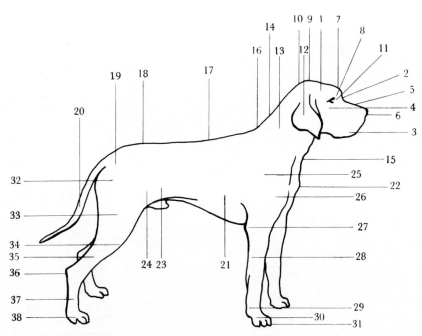

Fig. 2 **External Anatomy**:
1 skull, 2 stop, 3 muzzle, 4 cheek, 5 bridge of nose, 6 nose 7 forehead, 8 eye sockets, 9 crown, 10 occiput, 11 eye, 12 ear, 13 neck, 14 crest (nape), 15 throat, 16 withers, 17 back, 18 loin, 19 rump, 20 tail (in Hounds stern), 21 brisket, 22 chest, 23 belly, 24 flanks, 25 shoulder blade, 26 shoulder, 27 elbow, 28 forearm, 29 wrist, 30 pastern, 31 fore foot, 32 pelvis, 33 thigh, 34 stifle (knee), 35 second (or lower) thigh, 36 hock, 37 instep, 38 hind foot

 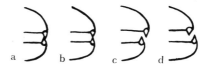

Fig. 3 **Dentition**:
Lower jaw: I incisors, C canines, P premolars, M molars. Bite: a) scissors bite, b) level bite, c) overshot, d) undershot

Thoroughbred appearance — the general impression the dog gives according to its breed and by which it can appear thoroughbred or not, over-bred with an unusually fine skeleton or too coarse.

Constitution — the dog's overall fitness, bearing in mind its physical structure, state of health and temperament, can be fine, coarse, lean or sluggish.

Condition — the physical state of the dog at a given moment, which can be described as good, moderate, poor, obese, emaciated, working, stud or show.

Terminology to describe individual parts of the body

Head can have thoroughbred or non-thoroughbred appearance, can be adequate, light, too heavy, coarse, reflects the dog's sex and is typical or non-typical.

Muzzle (fig. 4) can be long, short, pointed, blunt, narrow, broad.

Corners can be emphasized or not.

Lips can be fleshy, adequate, little developed, overhanging, close fitting, not close fitting, firmly closed.

Cheeks are bulging or flat.

Nose can be of various colours, nostrils can be narrow or broad.

Bridge of nose (fig. 5) can be level, convex, concave, broad or narrow.

Skull, as a whole, can be broad, narrow, long or short.

Stop (fig. 6), which forms the transition between the bridge of the nose and forehead, can be emphatic or slight, defined or not defined.

Forehead (fig. 7) is broad, narrow, flat, arched, domed, narrowing towards the eyes, with indentation (furrow) or without it.

Upper eye sockets are emphasized or not.

Crown can be broad, narrow, domed, flat, with or without indentation (furrow).

Occipital crest is perceptible, imperceptible, clearly defined or not.

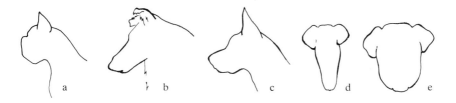

Fig. 4 **Muzzle**: a) short, b) long and pointed, c) blunt, d) narrow, e) broad

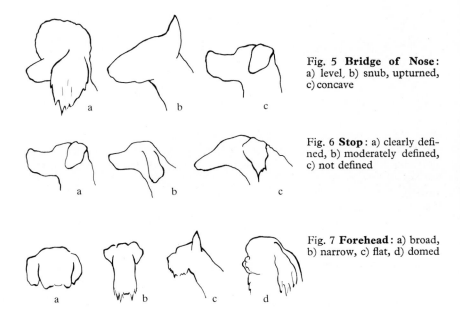

Fig. 5 **Bridge of Nose:**
a) level, b) snub, upturned,
c) concave

Fig. 6 **Stop:** a) clearly defined, b) moderately defined, c) not defined

Fig. 7 **Forehead:** a) broad,
b) narrow, c) flat, d) domed

Fig. 8 **Ear:** a) long, broad, with broad base, b) set low, pointed, c) set high, pointed, d) set low, long, with narrow base, e) set high, long, with broad base, f) small, pricked, pointed, g) small, fine, h) button, i) cropped

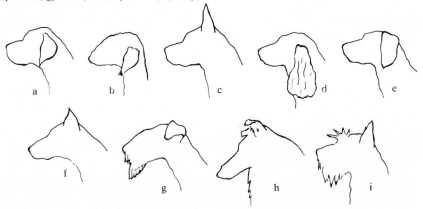

Eyes can be round, elliptical, triangular, almond-shaped, wide open, deep set, prominent, with raised or lowered lids. Their colour can be dark, dark brown, brown, hazel, light brown, amber, light, wild or fish-like. Expression can be lively, uncertain, calm, shy, fierce.

Ears (fig. 8) can be long or short, broad or narrow, small or large, set high or low, with narrow or broad base, fleshy, thin, pointed, rounded, erect (pricked), pendent, laying flat on cheeks or not, well or badly controlled, hanging to the side, dropped or semi-dropped (button), light, heavy cropped, post surgery (to correct some fault).

Fig. 9 **Neck**: a) arched, b) stag-like, c) set high, carried upright, d) set and carried low

Fig. 10 **Brisket**: Viewed from side: a) deep, long, b) shallow, c) deep, short. Viewed from front: d) barrel-shaped, e) flat

Fig. 11 **Rump and Tail Set**: a) rump level, tail set high, b) rump lowered, tail set low, c) rump level, tail set high, carried upright, d) rump sloping, tail set low, thick at root

Fig. 12 **Belly**:
a) tucked up, b) loose

Neck (fig. 9) can be described as long, short, weak, strong, adequate, muscular, slim, thick, set high or low, carried high or low, arched, stag-neck, ewe-neck.

Nape (the back of the neck) can be graceful, arched, short, long, muscular, broad, narrow.

Throat (the front of the neck) can be graceful, broad, narrow, clean cut, thick.

Brisket (fig. 10) can be deep, shallow, narrow, broad, short, long, barrel-shaped, humped, arched, well developed, pressed against the shoulders; viewed from the front it can be well developed, under-developed, flat, broad, narrow, well or poorly muscled.

Chest — brisket from the front — can be well or under-developed, flat, narrow, muscular or otherwise.

Shoulder (withers) can be described as high, low, well defined, not well defined.

Back can be level, roached, projecting, firm, soft, narrow, broad, long, short, poorly or adequately muscled.

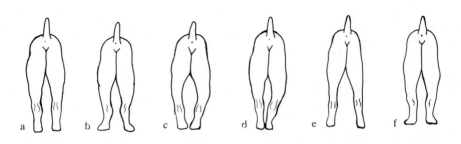

Fig. 13 **Posture of Hind Legs**: Viewed from back: a) normal, b) cow-hocked, c) barrel-legged, d) narrow, e) broad, f) diverging

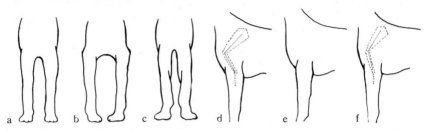

Fig. 14 **Posture of Forelegs**: Viewed from front: a) normal, b) converging, elbows turned outwards, c) diverging, elbows turned inwards. Viewed from side: d) normal, well bent, sloping shoulders, e) shallow instep, f) steep

Loin can be long, short, firm, soft, broad, narrow, well knit or loosely knit, well muscled or not, arched.

Flanks are broad, narrow, firm, loose, sunken, well filled.

Rump (fig. 11) — the rear part of the body from the crest of the hips to the seat — can be level, sloping, drooping, steep, long, short, broad, narrow, muscular or poorly muscled.

Pelvis can be described as oblique, steep, long, short, narrow, broad.

Hips can be projecting, clearly defined, not defined.

Tail (stern in the case of hounds) can be set high or low, can be thick, thin, coarse or fine, thick or thin at root, short, long, gradually tapering, docked short or rather longer, carried erect, in an arch or horizontally, downwards, curved, kinked, curled, curled over on back.

Hair on tail — long-haired gundogs can have a plume or feathering on the underside of tail, rough-haired varieties can have a brush.

Belly (fig. 12) is tucked up or loose, capacious or firm.

Anus not specified in detail.

Groin can be more or less fringed.

Genitalia not specified in detail.

Hind legs (fig. 13) can be straight, well or insufficiently bent, well or poorly muscled.

Thighs can be long, short, weak, strong, muscular or poorly muscled.

Trousers are formed by long hairs on back of hind legs and thighs.

Stifle (knee) can be free, turned out or turned in.

Lower or second thighs can be long, short, strong or weak.

Hocks are described as emphasized or not, narrow, broad, strong, weak, bare, well let down, high from the ground.

Heel can be long or short.

Pastern can be short, long, strong or weak, upright or bent under.

Feet are cat-like, hare-like, spoon-shaped, closed up, compact, soft, arched, small, large.

Toes of hind feet can be firm, loose, closed up, compact, arched, flat.

Dewclaws not specified in detail.

Nails or claws can be strong, weak, filed down, too long, colour can correspond to standard or not.

Forelegs (fig. 14) can be straight, crooked, rickety, well or badly bent, well or poorly muscled.

Shoulder blades are sloping, steep, long, short, firm, loose, according to the standard.

Shoulder joint is clearly or only slightly perceptible.

Upper arm is long or short.

Elbow is firm, loose, turned in or turned out, flat.

Forearm can be long, short, strong, straight, crooked, rickety.

Trousers of forelegs are formed by longer hair on back of forearms in long-haired breeds.

Pastern can be strong, weak, emphasized or not, rickety.

Instep can be long, short, firm, soft, steep, regularly or irregularly bent.

Feet as in the case of hind feet.

Toes as in the case of hind feet.

Dewclaws not specified in detail.

Nails or claws as in the case of hind feet.

Colour of coat can vary according to the provisions of the standard.

Quality of coat is constituted by the undercoat and outercoat. These together with the colour create the typical coat for the breed determined by the standard. It can be short, long, wavy, curly, straight, coarse, fine, close, open, hard, soft, glossy, mat, harsh, smooth, dense or sparse. It can have bald patches or be moulting, well or badly trimmed or clipped.

Eyebrows — a characteristic feature of rough-haired breeds — can be strong, weak, emphasized, not emphasized, perceptible, imperceptible.

Beard and whiskers — also a feature of rough-haired breeds — can be well developed, adequately, over- or under-developed.

Posture and gait. At shows not only the shape of the legs and their muscles are described but also their posture in repose and in action. Judges, therefore, insist on seeing the dog in action in order to assess the qualities or faults of the legs which influence the whole mechanism of movement.

Posture of forelegs (fig. 14) can be correct, narrow, broad, close-set, wide-set, converging or diverging, correctly or incorrectly bent.

Posture of hind legs (fig. 13) can be normal, steep, cow-hocked, barrel-shaped, set under, converging, diverging, standing firmly, broad, narrow, correctly or incorrectly bent.

Gait when walking can be solid and firm, light, flexible, short-stepped, long-stepped, heavy.

Gait when trotting or galloping can be light, flexible, short, solid or heavy.

Incorrect gait occurs when fore and hind legs on same side move forward simultaneously.

Temperament of the dog. At shows the judges must also ascertain whether the dog's disposition is in accordance with the standard. The dog may be described as being full of character, straightforward, crafty, good, bad, wild, gentle, fearless, timid, trustful, mistrustful.

At the Dog Show

It is the endeavour of every breeder to reproduce dogs which approach as nearly as possible the ideal described in the standard. To what extent these endeavours are successful can be seen at dog shows where the external appearance of the dog is evaluated by qualified judges.

In individual countries, shows are organized by the governing bodies for dog breeding such as the Kennel Club in Great Britain. On the European continent, in Latin America and parts of Africa where the dog breeding authorities belong to the FCI (Fédération Cynologique Intenationale), regional, national, special and international shows are held under FCI rules.

Almost everywhere breeds are separated for show purposes into two main divisions: Sporting and Non-sporting breeds, the former covering Hounds, Gundogs and Terriers, the latter Utility, Working and Toy dogs. In the case of each breed there are further sub-divisions according to sex, age, whether they have passed certain tests, holders of titles and so on. In Britain, under Kennel Club rules, only the best dogs in each class receive acknowledgement whereas, under FCI rules, every dog exhibited is given a mark: Excellent, for the best, Very Good, Good, and so on. At some shows the title 'Class Victor' is also given to the best dog and bitch in the class. At international shows in FCI countries, the best dog and bitch of each breed may be given the CACIB award (Certificat d'Aptitude au Championat International de Beauté). A dog or bitch which receives the required number of CACIB awards in the course of not less than one year, from different judges and in different countries, can become an 'International Champion'.

A similar rule applies to championship shows held in Britain under Kennel Club regulations. A dog has to be awarded three challenge certificates under three different judges to become a champion. Only dogs which are former champions or which have won first or second place at championship shows are eligible to appear at Britain's supreme dog show — Crufts.

Titles are noted in the dog's pedigree as are marks awarded in FCI countries, with the result that the dog concerned and his or her progeny become more valuable.

Getting Ready for a Show

If a dog is to do well at a show it must be in what is termed 'show condition'. That means it must be in good health and well muscled, neither too fat nor too thin. It must be well cared for which means, among other things, that its coat must be well prepared. Getting a dog ready for a show should start at least three months ahead and, in the case of long- or rough-haired dogs, even earlier.

When preparing for a show begin by seeing that the dog is correctly nourished and that its coat is growing as it should. The dog must be groomed daily with a metal comb. Short-haired and some long-haired dogs require daily brushing to remove the dying undercoat and moulting hairs on the surface so that the coat lies correctly. This regular massaging of the skin promotes new growth.

For the majority of short-haired breeds this is enough, though from time to time the dog should be bathed and washed in warm water. Use a good mild soap or shampoo and afterwards rinse the dog thoroughly with clean water and dry it well.

The coats of long-haired breeds require additional care so that the elegance of certain parts of the body will be shown off to best advantage and so that the dog will conform to the required standard. Setters, hunting spaniels, German pointers and Wachtelhunds (German spaniels) for example usually require nothing more than to have overlong and moulting hair stripped with the fingers from those parts of the body for which the standard requires shorter hair. Scissors should be used to tidy up long hair from around the feet so that these acquire the desired shape. Bathing long-haired dogs demands particular care. Bathing dries up the oil from the coat and makes it fluffy and unmanageable so that it curls or becomes too wavy. A long-haired dog should therefore be bathed not less than a week before the show so that there is enough time for the coat to be brushed and combed in the right direction and to settle down.

Similar care should be devoted to rough-haired dogs, but most of them need their coats trimmed and tailored to give them the typical form and appearance.

The exhibitor must choose the right time to start work on preparing the coat so that on the day of the show it is of the prescribed length and texture on individual parts of the body.

The coat is dealt with either by clipping or stripping. The method used is dependent on the texture of the coat as laid down in the standard. Various tools are necessary such as dog clippers, stripping knives, scissors and metal combs.

A dog can be stripped only when its coat is ripe for it, that is to say when it begins to moult. At this stage the coat can be stripped without much difficulty and without entailing pain for the dog. To try to strip a coat that is not yet ready for it is a difficult and — for the dog — a painful process.

To ensure that the coat will be in a show condition, the 'hairdressing' is done stage by stage so that it reaches the length required by the standard for different parts of the body at exactly the right time. Stripping cannot be replaced by clipping because clipping makes the hair soft and causes it to lose its characteristic texture. The timing of the various stages is individual, depending on how quickly each dog's coat grows. Some dog's coats grow slowly (especially in spring), the coats of others grow quickly (particularly in autumn). The directions that follow for preparing the coats of several breeds are therefore only approximate and the rate at which the coat grows must be ascertained individually for each dog.

Grooming the Individual Breeds

Wire-haired Fox Terrier

A Fox Terrier in show form should have its coat trimmed to a different length on different parts of its body. Apart from the beard and legs which are not stripped as a rule, the longest hair should be on the back, where it should be 3—3.5 cm long. On the sides of the body and the sides of the neck it should be 1—1.5 cm long and on the head and ears only a few millimetres. The transition from one part of the body to another should be inconspicuous so that the dog looks as if it has been sculptured. This is achieved by gradually stripping various sections of the coat step by step. Start stripping on the parts where the coat should be longest, leaving till last the places where the coat is to be shortest. The individual areas shown in the illustration should be dealt with as follows:

Areas 1, 2 and 3: Trimming should begin here. At least three months before the show, the hair on the legs is combed upwards and individual overgrown hairs, especially on the back of the thighs are stripped with the fingers so that the coat will grow thicker and richer to give the legs the appearance of regularly shaped pillars. The stripping should not be overdone for the hair on the legs grows very slowly. At the same time start regular daily combing in a forward direction of all the hair on the muzzle in order to 'elongate' the head. No opportunity should be lost for accustoming the coat for this position. However, care must be taken to see that the hair on the muzzle is not damaged.

Area 4: This entire area should be stripped very thoroughly to an even length about eight weeks before the show. In the case of dogs whose coats grow quickly six weeks is sufficient for the hair to grow again to the correct length.

Area 5: The trimming of this area depends on the shape of the brisket of the individual dog. If the brisket is flat and the abdomen is well held in, the trimming can be done earlier (about five to six weeks before the show), while work should start on a dog with a well developed brisket a week later. The coat should be well stripped but not to a state of near nakedness.

Area 6: Stripping the tail must start four weeks prior to the show. The entire tail should be carefully stripped, more being taken from the underneath than from the sides and the upper surface, so that from the root to the tip it will be of the same thickness.

Area 7: The shoulders, chest and the sides of the neck should be well trimmed four weeks before the show.

Area 8: The bridge of the nose, the space between the eyes, around inner eye corners and under the eyes should be gently stripped three weeks before the show to give the impression of the head being longer. However, the stripping should not be done so closely that the beard and moustache are reminiscent of the head of a poodle.

Area 9: The forehead and crown should be thoroughly stripped (of undercoat, too) two weeks before the show. Above the upper curve of the eye sockets the original hair should be left only being stripped gently to produce the characteristic terrier eyebrows.

Area 10: About ten to twelve days before the show, this area should be stripped as close as practicable so that the head will appear as narrow as possible. Where the outer corners of the eyes and the corner of the mouth approach there should be a smooth transition between the completely trimmed area 10 and the partially trimmed area 8.

Area 11: Exceptional care must be paid to the Fox Terrier's ears. The entire surface of the ear — both outer and inner — should be very gently stripped. In the case of particularly sensitive dogs or if the coat is not yet ripe for stripping, clippers may be used on the ears or at any rate overgrown hairs on the edges of the ears may be removed with scissors. Small, light-weight ears must be stripped two weeks before the show, so that when the day arrives they have recovered from the irritating effect of stripping and fall naturally in their correct position. Larger, heavier ears may be stripped only a week before the show and at the same time the edges should be trimmed to make them appear smaller.

Area 12: The throat of the Fox Terrier is carefully stripped ten to twelve days before the show so that the neck has a graceful line.

Area 13: This is where dogs are most sensitive so careful trimming should be done

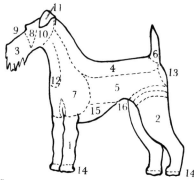

Fig. 15 Trimming a Rough-haired Fox Terrier

with clippers a week before the show. The resulting impression is that the dog is shortened.

Area 14: Here it is only a matter of shortening overgrown hairs so that the feet appear small, round and cat-like and form the continuation of the solid 'pillars'. Trimming is done with scissors or stripping with the fingers a week before the show.

Area 15: The hair on the underside of the brisket is combed in a downward and forward direction while any hair that is moulting is combed out. Excessively long hair is stripped with the fingers about a week before the show to form a smooth transition to the closely stripped abdomen. The hair that is left is intended to give the impression of a deep brisket, but this should not be exaggerated.

Area 16: The belly and flanks are thoroughly stripped with the fingers a week before the show. In the case of very sensitive dogs this part of the body can be trimmed with clippers or scissors.

The last week before the show is devoted to final tidying up. Special care should be taken not to leave any obvious transitions between the individual areas which have been stripped in different stages. Meticulous attention should be paid to the final tidying up of the beard and whiskers and the hair of the legs, particularly that of the thighs. The transition between the short hair on the flanks and the long hair on the thighs and shins must be uninterrupted and smooth. This can be achieved by using a comb to blend the fluffed up hair on the thighs with the shorter hair. The same applies to the front legs at the elbow. It is not elegant to leave too much roughed up hair on the thighs. In the upper part of the thighs the muscles should stand out. The impression of a low hock is increased by the regular upward combing of the hair and the careful plucking out of any excessive hairs so that the hind legs form pillars similar to the front legs.

A week before the show the dog should be bathed and should not be allowed to get dirty again. The day before the show it should be rubbed down thoroughly with a damp cloth so that the hairs of the coat will not separate out again. Then a brush should be used for another thorough grooming. The coat is greatly improved if, after grooming with a metal comb, it is smoothed over with a flannel.

Smooth-haired Fox Terrier
The coat of the Smooth-haired Fox Terrier demands far less attention than that of its wire-haired cousin. In theory the coat needs no special care at all. However, there are few Smooth-haired Fox Terriers with absolutely perfect coats and most of them require

attention to certain parts of the body so that overgrown hairs do not spoil the graceful line.

In most cases it is necessary to trim the throat and tidy up what is known as the 'collar' at the sides of the neck. It is also necessary to trim away excess hair (known as a frill or trousers) on the hind side of the thighs and to treat the tail in a similar way to that of a Wire-haired Fox Terrier.

All this must be inconspicuous so as to achieve a smooth transition between trimmed and untrimmed parts. It should therefore be done about three weeks before the show.

Clippers or scissors should only be used on the abdomen. Elsewhere scissors should not be used at all, because any cutting away of the coat can be seen at a first glance and completely disfigures the appearance of a Smooth-haired Fox Terrier.

Welsh Terrier, Irish Terrier and Airedale Terrier
Welsh, Irish and Airedale Terriers should be treated in the same way as Wire-haired Fox Terriers.

Scottish Terrier
Area 1: This is plucked by hand — and only if actually necessary — at least six months before the show so that long flowing hair will grow on this part of the body. Otherwise the coat is simply combed downwards and moulting hair from the undercoat is removed.

Area 2: This part should be thoroughly stripped eight to ten weeks before the show.

Area 3: At the same time this area is trimmed with clippers, since it is a part of the body particularly sensitive to stripping.

Area 4: The tail is thoroughly stripped about eight weeks before the show, and about fourteen days prior to the show it should be tidied up so that it is well-grown and cone-shaped.

Area 5: This area is completely stripped about a fortnight before the show. Eyebrows are left above each eye, separated from each other by a parting between the eyes. The trimming is done in such a way that the hair is shortest at the outer corner of each eye and as long as possible at the inner corners. At the root of each ear a tuft of longer hair is left at the front. Apart from this the ears are clipped.

Area 6: The Scottish Terrier's beard is its greatest adornment and continual care should be taken of it. After every meal the whiskers should be wiped with a damp cloth and combed forward so that energetic combing to remove the dry remains of food, which could damage it, is unnecessary.

Fig. 16 Trimming a Scottish Terrier

Area 7: All that is necessary is to trim away any overgrown hairs. But the feet should not be modelled by clipping.

Czech Terrier

This dog is clipped for the first time at the age of three to four months. It can be clipped with ordinary scissors because the steps thus formed help to achieve the desired waviness of the new hair.

It is best to start clipping from the tip of the tail and work forward along the back and sides of the body to the head. The tail and the area around the anus are clipped short. The longer hair on the legs and underside of the abdomen is left at its original length, only being slightly shortened if it is excessively long, the length being adjusted so that the body of the dog is barrel-shaped.

The chest and throat are trimmed short and so are the entire head and ears. Rather long eyebrows are left (these protect the eyes) and a moustache and beard are left on the upper and lower jaws, that is on the facial part of the head. These whiskers give the head its brick-like shape though they should not be too long. The lower jaw is otherwise trimmed from the throat right up to the lips.

New hair grows to show condition in one and a half to two months; there are, of course, individual differences in the rate at which the coat grows.

In winter or cold weather, Czech Terriers can be left with longer coats. It is worth noting that the quality of the coat — its waviness and texture — goes on improving as the dog grows older. Clippers may be used but clipping should be done in the direction in which the coat grows.

Clipping the coat has the advantage over other methods, such as stripping, because the owner can trim the dog whenever he needs to, even just a few hours before the show. Of course, the coat should not be clipped short but to the length laid down in the standard.

Before the show the Czech Terrier can be bathed. Immediately before it goes into the ring, the hair on the head and body should be rubbed down with a damp cloth, working from the back forwards to ensure that the coat has the correct form. The beard and longer hair on the body and legs are groomed with a metal comb — downwards in the case of the legs and abdomen, forwards in the case of the beard and eyebrows.

Bedlington Terrier

The Bedlington Terrier is either trimmed with clippers or scissor-trimmed through a comb. The trimming is a comparatively simple matter but requires a thorough knowledge of the standard and a talent for fine modelling. All transitions between hair of different lengths must be smooth and inconspicuous.

Area 1: This part does not have to be cut but should be groomed daily against the grain to ensure that the hair stands up. The hair on the brisket is combed down to give the impression of greater depth.

Area 2: This part should be trimmed short with clippers or with scissors through a comb about six weeks before the show.

Area 3: This comprises the lower jaw, cheeks and throat and is separated from surfaces 1 and 2 by a dividing line joining the corner of the mouth, the outer corner of the eye, the front of the base of the ear, the back of the base of the ear and the depression between the shoulders. This area is trimmed short with clippers a week before the show.

Area 4: The entire ear, outside and in, is trimmed short with clippers a week before the show, except for the tip. This is left uncut to encourage the growth of long tassels. The tip is sharply defined from the rest of the ear, forming a right-angled triangle; the tip of the triangle lies along the lengthwise axis of the ear at a distance of 2.5 cm from the end of the ear.

Area 5: The tail and the surroundings of the anus should be clipped a week before the show, while at the same time scissors and comb should be used to achieve a smooth blending of the clipped area with the neighbouring longer hair.

Area 6: The abdomen and flanks should be trimmed very short with clippers a week before the show while at the same time scissoring should blend this area with the neighbouring longer hair.

Area 7: Three weeks before the show the toes should be carefully trimmed with scissors. Scissors should also be used to ensure smooth blending with the uncut hair on the legs.

Immediately prior to the show, scissors and comb should be used to smooth away all sharp transitions (except in the case of the tips of the ears) and the whole body should be modelled into the desired shape. Special care should be devoted to the head with its characteristic topknot so that — seen from the front — it should appear like a long, narrow, blunt wedge.

Fig. 17 Trimming a Bedlington Terrier   Fig. 18 Trimming a Kerry Blue Terrier

Kerry Blue Terrier

The Kerry Blue Terrier is not stripped but trimmed. Work should begin on the coat according to how quickly it grows, that is from two to six weeks before the show. On the actual day of the show the hair on the back should be about 2 cm long.

Area 1: This is trimmed short with clippers. Begin on the ears and work down to the crown, temples and throat. The hair on the edges of the ears should be scissor-trimmed.

Area 2: Trim this part through a comb with scissors. Begin from the tip of the tail and continue against the grain up to the crown. This should be done by taking tufts of hair with the comb and snipping off the hair close to the teeth of the comb. Take only a small part at a time and always cut at the same distance so that there are no ugly transitions.

Area 3: Trim close with clippers.

Area 4: The hair on the underside of the brisket and on the legs is not clipped but only carefully combed in a downward direction.

Area 5: The beard and moustache of the Kerry Blue Terrier which are exceptionally large are cared for in a similar way as those of the Scottish Terrier. The hair making up the eyebrows is only clipped away from the sides of the eyes sufficiently to enable the dog to see well.

Area 6: The feet are scissor-trimmed very carefully to shorten any overgrown hair which would make the feet appear unnecessarily large.

The transition between individual areas should be smooth and well-blended and just before the show the dog should be finally tidied up with scissors through a comb.

Poodle

The poodle is not stripped but clipped. The standard permits two alternative methods of trimming the coat — the classical and the modern. It is up to the exhibitor to make the choice. The modern trim is not seen in the show ring in America or Great Britain except on puppies.

Classical Trim

For a long time the classical trim was regarded as the only permissible one conforming with the standard. It is also known as the 'lion' cut.

Area 1: The fore- and hind feet, including the surface of the toes and between the toes, are carefully trimmed with clippers and scissors. The same method is used for trimming the part behind the toes of the forefeet and the hocks of the hind feet up to the ankle joint.

Area 2: This area is either trimmed short with clippers up to the elbow joint, or the hair is left and is only trimmed with scissors to an even length to ensure a smooth line and give the legs the appearance of pillars.

Area 3: This part of the front legs (if area 2 has been clipped short) and of the hind legs forms a cuff which goes round the wrist or ankle. Scissors are used to trim them into the shape of barrels.

Area 4: The hocks, thighs and rump and the part of the body up to the last ribs are smoothly clipped to a short even length.

Area 5: The tail is clipped only for a third of its length from the root. The remainder is left uncut and is only shaped with scissors into a round or curved pompon.

Area 6: This part is not clipped at all, only tidied up with scissors to remove any overgrown hairs and to give it a smooth form.

Area 7: The lower jaw down to the throat and the bridge of the nose up to the stop are clipper-trimmed to a short length; the clipped part can extend beyond the line joining the eyes by a maximum of 1 to 2 cm. The cheeks are trimmed with clippers and scissors as far as the inner edge of the ear so that the ears can hang gracefully from the head. The eyes are cleared by trimming away any overgrown hairs while the head is being generally tidied up. A heavy moustache is left on the upper lip.

Area 8: The ears are shaped with scissors by trimming away any overgrown hairs to form a smooth shape and create a harmonious entity of the whole head.

Modern Trim

The modern trim has been permissible for the CACIB International Beauty Award only since 1965 when a new standard for the poodle was first issued in which the modern or '1960' trim was first described.

Area 1: The hair on the throat and upper and lower jaws and the hair on the bridge of the nose up to the stop is trimmed short with clippers. The hair on the feet is cut short: on the front feet it is either cut from the claws up to the dewclaws or just on the feet alone while the hair on the hind legs is trimmed to a corresponding height. The feet thus protrude from the fur as though from baggy trousers.

A moustache is permitted but must not extend beyond the lower jaw by more than 1 cm. A 'Billy goat's beard' on the chin is permissible at shows.

Area 2: The hair on the back is scissor-trimmed to a length of from 0.5 to 1 cm.

Areas 3 and 4: In this area the shortest hair blends into the longest. The transition must be modelled sensitively with no sharp breaks. The trimmed part converges on a line leading vertically upwards from the underside of the abdomen. Viewed from the side, the line leading along the inner perimeter of the legs and the underside of the belly resembles the letter A.

Area 5: The hair on the head, ears, legs and the tip of the tail is not cut, only the tips of overgrown hairs being trimmed into the shape required. The head, which is known as the 'topknot' or 'cap' and the tail form egg-shaped pompons. Alternatively the tip of the tail may be trimmed a little more so that it does not have a noticeable pompon.

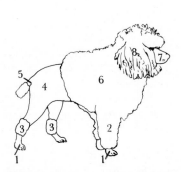

Fig. 19 Poodle — Classical Trim

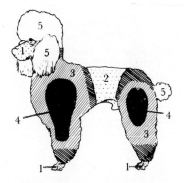

Fig. 20 Poodle — Modern Trim

The numbers following the dog's name relate to A Brief Guide
to Identification of Individual Breeds (p. 150)

Great Swiss Mountain Sheepdog   112

The largest of the Swiss dogs.
General Appearance: Large, strong, harmoniously built, a shaggy dog with pendent ears and long tail.
Head: Powerful but by no means clumsy, skull broad and flat, muzzle moderately long, stop only slightly defined. Jaws strong, scissors bite. Nose black. Eyes medium-sized, hazel or chestnut brown. Ears moderately large, set high, triangular, in repose lying flat, well coated with hair.
Neck: Strong, moderately long, well muscled with no dewlap.
Body: Back moderately long, strong and straight. Brisket deep and broad, loins strong and broad, rump broad and long.
Legs and Feet: Forelegs long, shoulder blades strong and slanting, joining the shoulder in a blunt angle; thighs strong. Feet compact.
Tail: Rather heavy, in repose held low, in action somewhat raised but never curling over the back.
Coat: Lying close to the body, guard hairs 3—5 cm long.
Colour: Basic colour black and tan and white symmetrical markings.
Height and Weight: Dogs 65—70 cm, bitches 60—65 cm; weight not officially prescribed.
Origin of Breed: Descended from types bred for many centuries in isolated Swiss valleys.
Characteristics and Uses: Intelligent, wary, courageous, affectionate to own family, easy to manage, quiet, not inclined to roam, proven to be a good guardian of herds and an agreeable companion.

Bernese Mountain Dog   109

Most widespread of Swiss herding dogs.
General Appearance: Large, sturdy but not clumsy, long-haired dog with drop ears and long, well covered tail.
Head: Large with flat skull and scarcely perceptible stop, muzzle straight and strong, scissors bite. Nose black. Eyes dark brown, almond-shaped. Ears moderately large, set high, triangular, falling close to the head when in repose.
Neck: Moderately long, strong, well muscled and well covered with hair.
Body: Back moderately long, firm, and straight, chest broad and deep, loins strong.
Legs and Feet: Well muscled, forelegs straight, shoulders long and sloping, thighs broad and strong, hocks well bent, broad and strong. Feet short, round and compact.
Tail: Thickly coated with hair, reaching to below the hock joint, slightly plumed.
Coat: Long, straight or slightly wavy.
Colour: Basic colour deep black with tan markings on the cheeks, eyebrows, legs and chest. Symmetrical blaze and white marking on the chest desirable.
Height and Weight: Dogs 64—70 cm, bitches 58—66 cm; weight not officially prescribed.
Origin of Breed: Swiss breed from the neighbourhood of Berne, possibly descended from the Molossian Dog.
Characteristics and Uses: Intelligent, watchful and very affectionate dog. Ideal family dog which can adapt itself to town life if given sufficient exercise. Excellent watchdog and, of course, a good draught dog that being the purpose for which it was bred.

Pyrenean Mountain Dog   119

Spanish breed of guard and herding dog.

General Appearance: Dog of great size, substance and power with moderately long coat, flat ears and long, thickly haired tail.

Head: Not too heavy in proportion to size of dog. Muzzle strong, of medium length. Nose black. Scissors bite. Eyes almond-shaped, dark amber-brown, somewhat obliquely set. Ears fairly small, triangular, with rounded tips, the base being on a level with the eyes, lying flat against the head.

Neck: Fairly short, thick and muscular, covered with long hair.

Body: Back of good length, broad, muscular, straight and level. Rump slightly downward sloping. Chest broad and deep. Dogs have more pronounced waist than bitches.

Legs and Feet: Forelegs strong, straight, well plumed. Thighs long, heavily muscled, tapering gradually down to the hocks. The stifle and hock joints should have only medium angulation. Double dewclaws on hind legs. Feet short and compact.

Tail: Thick at root, should be long enough to reach the hocks, abundantly covered with long hair which should form a plume. In repose carried low, when alert curled high above the back.

Coat: Profuse fine undercoat, outercoat coarser, thick and straight or slightly wavy.

Colour: Mainly white, may have patches of badger, wolf grey or pale yellow on ears, head and around tail root.

Height and Weight: Dogs 70—80 cm, bitches rather less; 45—55 kg.

Origin of Breed: Descended from original breed.

Characteristics and Uses: Intelligent, independent, good natured, but also wary. Is a good watchdog or herding dog and a faithful companion for those who can give it sufficient exercise.

Caucasian Sheepdog   118

There are three varieties of this sheepdog which comes from the Soviet Union: long-haired, short-haired and dogs of a middle type. Those which actually come from the Caucasian region are more powerfully built than the steppeland variety which is lighter and taller.

General Appearance: Medium-sized to large dog of massive, muscular build.

Head: Powerful. Skull broad, forehead broad and flat, stop only slight. Muzzle pointed, lips thick, scissors bite. Nose large, broad and black, brown in the case of white or light brown dogs. Eyes small, oval. Ears drooping or erect, sometimes cropped short.

Neck: Well set on shoulders, rather muscular and arched.

Body: Brisket well developed, belly and flanks firm, thighs well muscled.

Legs and Feet: Straight, well muscled.

Tail: Docked or un-docked.

Coat: Outercoat straight and rough, undercoat dense. In long-haired types it forms a collar round the neck. In the medium type it is long and straight but forms no collar.

Colour: Grey, white, brown, light tan, brindle or roan.

Height and Weight: Dogs 65—80 cm, bitches at least 65 cm; weight not officially prescribed (about 50 kg).

Origin of Breed: Descended from original breed.

Characteristics and Uses: Fierce, suspicious of strangers. Can stand up to harsh winter weather. Good herding and watchdog.

Polish Tatra Sheepdog (Owczarek Podhalański) 113

Polish breed of herding dog similar to the Hungarian Kuvasz and the Slovakian Chuvach.
General Appearance: Large white dog with profuse coat. Dogs' coat is slightly shorter than bitches'.
Head: Clean in outline. Skull slightly domed, stop clearly defined, muzzle strong with wide bridge. Scissors bite. Nose black. Eyes moderately large, rather obliquely set. Ears moderately long, triangular, thick, with profuse hair.
Neck: Moderately long, muscular, no dewlap. Profuse curly collar.
Body: Long and massive. Back straight, broad, withers clearly defined, broad, rump slightly sloping, brisket deep, belly slightly tucked up.
Legs and Feet: Forelegs muscular with strong but not too heavy bones, shoulder blades somewhat slanting. Hind legs moderately bent, set rather far back. Thighs covered with long coat. Feet comparatively large, oval with hair between toes.
Tail: Set not too high, carried below the level of the back, profusely coated.
Coat: On neck and body long, thick, straight or slightly wavy. On head and muzzle short.
Colour: White only.
Height and Weight: Dogs 65—70 cm, bitches 60—65 cm; weight not officially prescribed.
Origin of Breed: Descended from original breed.
Characteristics and Uses: Very intelligent, faithful, affectionate and good-natured with children. Well-tried herding and watchdog and pleasant companion. Needs plenty of space. Coat requires careful attention.

Kuvasz 106

A breed of herding dog from the mountains of Hungary.
General Appearance: Large strong dog with a wavy white coat, drop ears and a long tail carried down.
Head: Skull rather long, forehead long and only slightly domed, slight stop, muzzle broad and long, scissors bite. Nose black. Eyes obliquely set, almond-shaped, dark. Ears set high, V-shaped, pendent but inclined to stand out from the head.
Neck: Moderately long, strong, with no loose skin.
Body: Withers long and higher than back, back moderately long, brisket deep, long and somewhat flattened, rump slanting slightly downwards, belly slightly tucked up.
Legs and Feet: Forelegs straight, hind legs well muscled and firmly set. Feet compact, toes arched.
Tail: Long, set deep, carried slightly raised with the tip turning gently upwards, covered with dense, fairly long hair.
Coat: On head, ears, feet and front of legs short, elsewhere fairly long and slightly wavy, well feathered tail.
Colour: White.
Height and Weight: Dogs at least 65 cm, bitches at least 60 cm; weight not officially prescribed.
Origin of Breed: Probably the result of crossing original breed with the Molossian Dog and the Komondor.
Characteristics and Uses: Intelligent, decorative, reliable, faithful, suspicious of strangers. Good herding and watchdog. Has recently become popular as a house dog. Needs a great deal of exercise.

Polish Lowland Sheepdog (Polski Owczarek Nizinny) 60

Polish herding dog which looks rather like a bear cub.

General Appearance: Medium-sized, long-haired dog with naturally short or docked tail.

Head: Moderately large but not too heavy, clearly defined stop, scissors or level bite. Nose black. Eyes medium-sized, oval, hazel-coloured. Ears medium-sized, set fairly high, heart-shaped. Forehead, cheeks and beard profusely covered with hair.

Neck: Moderately long, muscular.

Body: Back level, well muscled, withers clearly defined, rump sloping slightly downwards, brisket deep and fairly broad, belly somewhat tucked in.

Legs and Feet: Straight, thighs well muscled. Feet oval.

Tail: Docked if not born with a stump.

Coat: Long and dense. Falls from the forehead over the eyes. Straight but may be slightly wavy.

Colour: All colours and markings of all colours are acceptable.

Height and Weight: Dogs 43—52 cm, bitches 40—46 cm; weight not officially prescribed.

Origin of Breed: Descended from an original type of sheepdog.

Characteristics and Uses: Intelligent, teachable, lively, does not roam, devoted to its own family but wary of strangers. Excellent at guarding herds and home. Suitable for places where it is not possible to keep a large dog. Not particularly exacting and apart from daily grooming needs no special care.

Komondor 124

Shepherds' dog from the plains of Hungary.

General Appearance: Large, imposing, muscular dog with long, shaggy white coat which tends to cord.

Head: Skull slightly arched, stop moderate, muzzle broad and rather coarse, not blunt or pointed, scissors bite. Nostrils wide, nose black. Lips tight fitting. Eyes medium-sized, dark, oval. Ears medium-sized, U-shaped and pendent.

Neck: Strong, muscular, moderately arched, medium length, richly coated, no dewlap.

Body: Broad, deep, muscular with back level, rump broad, sloping slightly. Because of the density of the dog's coat, withers are scarcely visible.

Legs and Feet: Forelegs like vertical columns, muscular, heavily coated. Hind legs strong and muscular, well angulated. Feet strong, large and compact.

Tail: Moderately long, set fairly high, coated with long hairs; reaches down to the hocks. Carried low, slightly curved at tip.

Coat: Long, dense and corded.

Colour: White.

Height and Weight: Dogs 65—85 cm, bitches 55—70 cm; dogs 50—60 kg, bitches 40—50 kg.

Origin of Breed: Probably from crossing the original breed with Molossian Dog and Kuvasz.

Characteristics and Uses: Quiet, very courageous and persistent dog, completely devoted to its master and suspicious of strangers. Typical herding dog, good watchdog and guard. Inclined to be pugnacious and therefore needs patient and calm handling. The coat requires considerable attention.

Hungarian Puli   50

Typical steppeland herding dog from the plains of Hungary.

General Appearance: Medium-sized dog with pendent ears, fairly long tail and long coat which tends to cord and felt.

Head: Fine, round head with slightly domed skull, well defined stop and straight muzzle, bluntly rounded at the nose. Nose large and black. Eyes dark brown, medium-sized. Ears set fairly high, V-shaped and pendent, covered with long hair.

Neck: Medium length, arched, tight and muscular.

Body: Withers slightly higher than level of back which is of medium length. Loin short, broad and tucked up. Chest deep and fairly broad. Rump slightly sloping.

Legs and Feet: Forelegs straight like pillars, muscular, vertical. Hind legs strong and well muscled, long-haired.

Tail: Moderately long, curled over the back, covered with long hair.

Coat: Long, thick, wavy and corded.

Colour: Black, rusty black, various shades of grey.

Height and Weight: Dogs 40—47 cm, bitches 37—44 cm; dogs 13—15 kg, bitches 10—13 kg.

Origin of Breed: Descended from original breed.

Characteristics and Uses: Striking in appearance, watchful, exceptionally mobile, devoted to its master but extremely suspicious of strangers. Makes a very good watchdog and sheepdog. Recently has also become popular as a house dog. Coat requires considerable attention. Enjoys barking.

Pumi   45

The most recently developed of the Hungarian sheepdog breeds.

General Appearance: Medium-sized, square-built dog with shaggy coat, ears with drooping tips, docked tail.

Head: Longish, crown domed, rather narrow, stop hardly perceptible, scissors bite. Nose longish and pointed. Eyes dark. Ears set high, held erect with drooping tips, medium-sized.

Neck: Moderately long, slightly arched, muscular.

Body: Withers long, back and loins short and well coupled, rump slightly sloping, brisket deep and long.

Legs and Feet: Forelegs straight, vertical, rather far apart, hind legs set fairly far forward. Feet firm and compact.

Tail: Set high, curled over hind quarters and docked if not born with stump of tail.

Coat: Moderately long, shaggy but not felted, leaving eyes and muzzle free.

Colour: All shades of grey, black, white and rusty brown.

Height and Weight: 35—45 cm; 8—13 kg.

Origin of Breed: Crossing of domestic breeds probably with Pomeranian Spitz.

Characteristics and Uses: Intelligent, modest, persistent, zealous in carrying out work entrusted to it, affectionate and devoted to its master. Satisfactory herding dog.

Bouvier de Flandres 86

French-Belgian breed of herding dog very similar to the Giant Schnauzer.
General Appearance: Moderately large, rough-coated dog of imposing appearance which reflects its courage and lively temperament.
Head: Moderately long, skull flat, somewhat broader than it is long, narrowing gradually at the muzzle, only slight stop, muzzle wide and strong, lips unwrinkled and flat, scissors bite. Eyes dark, slightly oval in shape. Ears set high, in Europe cropped to a V-shape, held erect, very mobile.
Neck: Fairly long and arched.
Body: Strong and muscular, back broad and short, straight and well muscled, shoulders and rump short and strong, brisket deep, not too wide.
Legs and Feet: Forelegs straight, shoulder blades long and sloping, hind legs well bent. Feet compact.
Tail: Set high, docked.
Coat: Very harsh, hard, dry, dull and tousled.
Colour: Dark fawn, pepper and salt, grey, dark brown.
Height and Weight: Dogs 58—65 cm, bitches 56—65 cm; dogs 35—40 kg, bitches 27—35 kg.
Origin of Breed: Descended from original breed.
Characteristics and Uses: Faithful, intelligent, teachable, wary, has strong nerves. Excellent herding and service dog.

Briard 99

The best known breed of French herding dogs.
General Appearance: Large, shaggy, rugged dog. In France and elsewhere on the continent of Europe its ears are cropped to stand erect.
Head: Strong, fairly long, slightly rounded forehead, stop clearly defined, muzzle neither narrow, nor pointed. Nose black, more square than round. Eyes rather large, dark, well opened. Ears set high, cropped.
Neck: Well muscled and arching, carried well away from the shoulders.
Body: Back firm and level, chest broad and well let down, a slight slope at the croup, belly slightly tucked up.
Legs and Feet: Well muscled, strong-boned, vertical, double dewclaws on hind legs. Feet strong and slightly rounded. Toes close together.
Tail: Long, well covered with hair. Carried low with an upward hook at the tip.
Coat: Long, slightly wavy and very dry (like the coat of a goat).
Colour: All solid colours except white. Darker shades preferred.
Height and Weight: Dogs 62—68 cm, bitches 56—64 cm; weight not officially prescribed.
Origin of Breed: There are various theories about the Briard's ancestry but it is probably related to the other shaggy-coated European sheepdogs.
Characteristics and Uses: Exceptionally teachable, quiet, watchful, agreeable, affectionate, sociable and happy dog, qualities which make it an excellent house dog. At the same time it is a good sheepdog, watchdog and service dog. It needs a good deal of exercise and its coat requires care.

Collie 78, 79

The most widespread of all British breeds of herding dog. Often regarded as the most beautiful of the canine race.

General Appearance: Large, slender, long-legged dog, elegant, with a long, very graceful head with a dreamy but at the same time alert expression, semi-prick ears and long, richly feathered tail.

Head: Skull flat, wedge-shaped, moderately wide between the eyes, gradually tapering to the end of the nose. Smooth, blunt but not square muzzle, perceptible but not prominent stop. Nose always black. Eyes medium-sized, somewhat obliquely set, almond-shaped, coloured dark brown except for merles when one or both eyes are frequently blue-white. Ears medium-sized, wide at the base, set not too close together, in repose carried thrown back, when alert semi-erect and forward with tips slightly drooping.

Neck: Muscular, powerful, arched.

Body: Rather long with well sprung ribs, deep chest, broad behind the shoulders, arched over the loins.

Legs and Feet: Forelegs straight and muscular, the elbows turning neither out nor in. Hind legs muscular at thighs, slender, sinewy, well angled. Feet oval, closed toes.

Tail: Fairly long, in repose carried low with an upward swirl at the end. In action carried gaily but never over the back.

Coat: Very dense, outercoat harsh, undercoat soft, furry, very close lying. Mane and frill abundant, face smooth. Forelegs well feathered, also the hind legs above the hocks. Shorter coat below the hocks.

Colour: Any colour acceptable and any markings.

Height and Weight: Dogs 56—61 cm, bitches 51—56 cm; dogs 20—30 kg, bitches 18—25 kg.

Origin of Breed: Descended from original breed with an admixture of Borzoi and Irish Setter blood.

Characteristics and Uses: Very intelligent, self-confident, keen, energetic, watchful, teachable dog. Devoted to its master, loves children and is a reliable house guard. Because of these qualities and its imposing appearance it is in great demand as a pet. Its coat needs regular care and the dog needs a great deal of exercise. Besides the illustrated rough-haired variety there is also the Smooth-haired Collie distinguished by very short, flat coat of harsh texture.

Shetland Sheepdog (Sheltie) 34

British breed, in appearance and disposition very similar to the Collie but considerably smaller.

General Appearance: Elegant, long-haired, keen dog.

Head: Skull flat, slightly widening between the ears and tapering towards the eyes, only slight stop. Muzzle rather long. Eyes medium-sized, oblique and almond-shaped, dark brown — though merle dogs have blue eyes. Ears small and erect with tips slightly drooping forwards.

Neck: Fairly long, muscular, arched.

Body: Long, back straight, well sprung ribs, deep chest, shoulders flat, front straight.

Legs and Feet: Forelegs straight, with strong bones, hind legs muscular, thighs well bent. Feet oval.

Tail: Fairly long, well feathered, in repose hangs down.

Coat: Outercoat long and straight; forms a mane round neck. Forelegs feathered, hind legs covered in dense hair.

Colour: Black and tan with white markings, merle, merle with white markings, sable with white markings.

Height and Weight: 35.5—36.8 cm; 6.5 kg.

Origin of Breed: The Shetland Sheepdog probably had common ancestors with the Collie but developed along different lines.

Characteristics and Uses: Elegant, gentle but alert dog, today more frequently a pet than a herding dog. Similar in disposition to the Collie. Coat needs regular attention.

Old English Sheepdog (Bobtail) 73

Typical family dog which looks something like a shaggy bear. Developed in England.
General Appearance: Medium-sized dog with profuse shaggy coat, thickset, muscular and well proportioned.
Head: Skull capacious and rather squarely formed, clearly defined stop, fairly long strong muzzle, scissors bite. Eyes dark or corresponding to the colour of the coat. Ears small, lying flat against the head.
Neck: Fairly long, arched gracefully and well coated with hair.
Body: Rather short and compact, brisket deep and wide, back straight, ribs well sprung, rump set higher than shoulders.
Legs and Feet: Forelegs straight, fairly long with strong bone. Hind legs well muscled with hocks well let down. Feet small and oval.
Tail: If necessary puppies' tails should be docked so that the tail of the adult dog will measure from 4 to 5 cm.
Coat: Profuse, hard and shaggy but free from curl.
Colour: Grey, grey roan, blue, blue roan with or without white markings.
Height and Weight: Dogs 56 cm and over, bitches slightly less; weight not officially prescribed.
Origin of Breed: The Bearded Collie was probably among its ancestors.
Characteristics and Uses: Intelligent, quiet, watchful but highly amenable. Because of its disposition and pleasant appearance, it is today more of a house dog than a sheepdog. Its love of children is proverbial. Coat needs a good deal of attention.

Pembroke Welsh Corgi 17

Smallest breed of herding dogs from Wales.
General Appearance: Low set but sturdily built dog, a little lower and slighter than its Cardigan cousin.
Head: Skull flat and fairly wide, foxy, moderate stop, muzzle powerful, slightly tapering, clean in outline, moderately long, lower jaw strong, scissors bite, strong teeth. Nose black. Eyes medium-sized, hazel, deep set and full of expression. Ears V-shaped, fairly large, set high, erect.
Neck: Muscular, fairly long and strong.
Body: Of medium length, level top line, brisket broad and deep, ribs well sprung, strongly marked withers, belly drawn in.
Legs and Feet: Shoulders long, sloping elbows fit close to the sides. Forelegs should aim straight ahead but should not be raised too much. Hind legs strong and well angled, thighs muscular, when viewed from behind the hocks should be straight and long. Feet small, oval, well arched and strong.
Tail: Short, preferably natural.
Coat: Medium length, dense, not wiry.
Colour: Any self colour but white acceptable, orange or pale yellow preferred. Other colours, however, sometimes occur.
Height and Weight: 25—30 cm; dogs 9—11 kg, bitches 8—10 kg.
Origin of Breed: Dog bred by Welsh farmers for herding. Originated in the County of Pembrokeshire in South Wales.
Characteristics and Uses: Intelligent, alert, very faithful. Needs no special care. Inclined to bark and has a tendency to nip the ankles. The **Cardigan Welsh Corgi** is somewhat heavier and has a long tail but the same characteristics.

The Boxer's head gives it the individual stamp peculiar to the breed. Developed in Germany.

General Appearance: Medium-sized, sturdy, smooth-haired lively dog of square build with strong legs which give it strength and speed.

Head: Clean in outline with no superfluous folds. The beauty of the head depends on the harmonious proportions of its parts. Viewed from any direction the muzzle should appear in correct relationship to the crown. The Boxer is normally undershot. Both jaws should be very wide in front. The lower edge of the thick upper lip should rest on the edge of the lower lip to fill out the space formed by the projection of the lower jaw. The chin must not rise above the front of the upper lip, but must be perceptible from front as well as from sides. The teeth of the lower jaw and the tongue should not be seen when the mouth is closed. Eyes should be dark brown with an energetic and intelligent expression. Ears set high and wide apart, in America and on the European continent cropped to a point.

Neck: Strong, round and muscular, should not be too thick and short. Marked nape and elegant arch down to the back. No dewlaps.

Body: Square in appearance. Chest should be deep reaching down to the elbows, ribs well sprung, tucked up loins. Back short and straight, broad, muscular. Pelvis long and, especially in bitches, it should be broad.

Legs and Feet: Forelegs seen from the front should be straight and parallel to each other and have strong, firmly jointed bones. Elbows should not press too close to the chest wall or stand off too far from it. Pastern should be short, and slightly slanting. Hind legs straight when viewed from the front, strongly muscled, musculation standing out. Thighs broad and curved. Croup slightly sloped, flat arched and broad. Small cat feet.

Tail: Set high, docked and carried upwards.

Coat: Short and shiny, smooth and close to the body.

Colour: Fawn (picture below), brindle and fawn in shades from light yellow (picture above) to dark deer red. The brindle Boxer should have black stripes on a golden-yellow or red-brown background. Stripes should be clearly defined, not very dense. White markings acceptable. Dark mask.

Height and Weight: Dogs 57—63 cm, bitches 53—59 cm; dogs about 30 kg, bitches about 25 kg.

Origin of Breed: The distant ancestors of the Boxer of today were dogs used for hunting bear, wolves and wild boar. The development of the Boxer has taken a comparatively long time and it was not recognized as a separate breed until 1925.

Characteristics and Uses: Faithful, quiet, clean and docile, but energetic and distrustful of strangers. Fearless as a defender and protector. A highly desirable family dog with an inborn love of children. At the same time an excellent guard and service dog. The short coat needs no special care.

Dobermann 114

German breed which possesses all the qualities required by a service dog, harmoniously combined with an elegant appearance.

General Appearance: A dog of good medium size with well set muscular, elegant body.
Head: Proportionate to the body. Seen from above and from the side resembles a blunt wedge. Muzzle should extend parallel to the topline of the skull. Nose black, lighter in the case of brown or blue dogs. Eyes as dark as possible. Ears small, set high, usually erect, cropped on the European continent.
Neck: Fairly long and lean, carried erect. Nape muscular.
Body: Square. Back short and firm with topline sloping slightly from the withers to the croup. Belly fairly well tucked up.
Legs and Feet: Forelegs perfectly straight and parallel to each other. Hind quarters well developed and muscular. Feet well arched and compact.
Tail: Should appear to be a continuation of the spine, docked at first or second joint.
Coat: Smooth, short, hard, thick and close lying.
Colour: Black, brown or blue with rusty red markings that should be clearly defined.
Height and Weight: Dogs 68—70 cm, bitches 63—66 cm; weight not officially prescribed.
Origin of Breed: From crossing the smooth medium-sized Pinscher with the Rottweiller and other breeds.
Characteristics and Uses: Faithful, intelligent, courageous, with strong nerves, amenable to training, nimble and quick, energetic and sharp. Good family friend and reliable service dog. Needs plenty of exercise and a firm hand from puppyhood.

Alsatian (German Shepherd) 89

One of the oldest breeds, widely used today as a service and police dog.
General Appearance: Well proportioned, larger dog, rather long and strongly boned, obviously capable of endurance, speed and quick and sudden movement.
Head: Long, lean and clean cut. Skull slightly domed, slight stop, muzzle strong and long. Teeth strong, scissors bite, lips tight fitting and clean. Nose black. Eyes almond-shaped, dark, with alert and intelligent expression. Ears of moderate size, placed high, carried erect with pointed tips.
Neck: Strong, fairly long with plenty of muscle, free from throatiness.
Body: Brisket deep, chest not too broad. Sides neither too flat nor barrel-shaped. Back broadish and straight, belly shows a waist without being tucked up. Loins broad and strong, rump long and sloping.
Legs and Feet: Shoulders sloping back, with plenty of muscle. Forelegs straight. Thighs broad and well muscled, stifles well turned, hocks strong and well let down. Feet round, toes strong, slightly arched and close together.
Tail: Thickly coated with hair. At rest should hang down to the hocks in a slight curve. In movement raised but not carried higher than a vertical line drawn through the base.
Coat: Can be of three kinds: short and hard, long and hard, long. Under the body to behind the legs the coat is longer and forms near the thigh a mild form of breeching.
Colour: Black, steel grey, ash grey, either solid coloured or with regular brown, yellow or greyish markings or can have a black saddle or can be wolf grey.
Height and Weight: Dogs 60—65 cm, bitches 55—60 cm; weight not officially prescribed.
Origin of Breed: The result of crossing various German herding dogs.
Characteristics and Uses: Full of character but at the same time adaptable and teachable, has strong nerves and is perpetually vigilant. Faithful and courageous, can be fierce. These qualities make it an admirable working dog, suitable for guard duties, protection and herding. Enthusiastic and happy worker. Not difficult to breed.

Exceptionally good guard and service dog of German breed.

General Appearance: Above average-sized stalwart dog whose bearing displays boldness and courage and gives the impression of strong individuality.

Head: Moderately long, skull broad between the ears. Occipital bone well developed, stop clearly defined. Eyes of medium size, dark brown in colour. Ears small in proportion, pendent, triangular.

Neck: Of fair length, strong and round and very muscular.

Body: Chest roomy, broad and deep. Back straight, strong and not too long. Croup broad and very slightly sloping.

Legs and Feet: Forelegs straight and not placed too closely together. Hind legs with fairly well bent stifles. Hocks well angulated without exaggeration and not completely vertical. Feet strong and round. Hind feet somewhat longer than forefeet.

Tail: Short, strong, not set too low, docked at first joint if naturally long.

Coat: Not very long, coarse and flat. The undercoat, required on the neck and thighs, must not show above the outercoat.

Colour: Black with clearly defined mahogany markings.

Height and Weight: Dogs 60—68 cm, bitches 55—63 cm; weight not officially prescribed.

Origin of Breed: Bred from a cattle dog which was popular with merchants and butchers as a droving and guard dog for their herds. The name is derived from that of the German town of Rottweil am Neckar.

Characteristics and Uses: Tranquil, watchful, faithful, very quick to learn and easily managed, fearless and persistent and enjoys working. Excellent guard and service dog. Requires gentle handling during training.

Giant Schnauzer   102

Large rough-haired dog, arousing respect. A German breed.

General Appearance: Large edition of the Standard Schnauzer (see p. 138).

Head: Strong and elongated, gradually narrowing from the ears to the eyes and thence forward to the tip of the nose. Medium stop to accentuate eyebrows. Powerful muzzle, bridge of nose straight, powerful jaws, scissors bite. Eyes medium-sized, dark, oval. Ears set high, drooping forward to temple, in many European countries cropped to a point.

Neck: Moderately long, nape strong and slightly arched, skin close to throat.

Body: Chest moderately broad, deep, with visible strong breast bone reaching down at least to the elbow and rising backwards to the loins. Back strong and straight with short, well developed loins. Ribs well sprung.

Legs and Feet: Strongly muscled. Forelegs straight with strong bone. Thighs slanting and flat. Feet short, round, extremely compact with close-arched toes.

Tail: Set and carried high, cut down to three joints.

Coat: Hard and wiry, just short enough for smartness. Bristly, stubby moustache and chin whiskers, arched bushy eyebrows.

Colour: Pure black or pepper and salt.

Height and Weight: Dogs 60—70 cm, bitches 60—65 cm; 30—35 kg. (Miniature Schnauzer 30—35 cm, 5—6 kg.)

Origin of Breed: The Schnauzer is derived from the rough-haired Giant Pinscher, very popular in the surroundings of Munich. Miniatures bred from smaller offspring of the Standard Schnauzer.

Characteristics and Uses: Good-natured with its own family, wary of strangers. Faithful, diligent and well suited to resist all weathers. Excellent service dog. Needs plenty of exercise. The Miniature Schnauzer is rather noisy. Excellent ratter.

Newfoundland 117

A dog of mastiff type but with a long coat.

General Appearance: Should give an appearance of great strength and activity.

Head: Broad and massive with well developed occipital bone and no decided stop. Muzzle short, clean cut and rather square in shape. Eyes small, dark brown, set rather wide apart. Ears small, set well back, lying close to the head with no fringe.

Neck: Strong, well set on shoulders and back.

Body: Back broad with strong muscular loins. Chest deep and fairly broad, well covered with hair.

Legs and Feet: Forelegs perfectly straight, muscular, feathered all the way down. Hind legs with great freedom of action, slightly feathered. Feet large and well shaped.

Tail: Moderately long, well covered with hair but with no flag. In repose hangs downwards with a slight curve at the end.

Coat: Flat and dense, rather coarse and oily to resist water.

Colour: Dull jet black. A slight tinge of bronze is acceptable.

Height and Weight: Dogs 68—75 cm, bitches 62—70 cm; dogs 50—62 kg, bitches 40—50 kg.

Origin of Breed: Brought by the British from Newfoundland to Europe where it was improved and refined.

Characteristics and Uses: Intelligent, gentle, faithful, docile dog, an excellent swimmer, not given to fighting or barking. Needs plenty of space and does not like hot weather. Excellent guard dog.

Leonberger 123

German breed outstanding for its majestic beauty and graceful appearance.

General Appearance: Large, strong, muscular, well proportioned dog, with small drop ears and long, profusely feathered tail.

Head: Held proudly, moderately domed, muzzle fairly long, slight stop, bridge of nose evenly broad, skin on head and face smooth and unwrinkled. Scissors bite. Eyes medium-sized, light to dark brown. Ears set high, lying flat, close to the head.

Neck: Moderately long.

Body: Somewhat longer than height at withers, back firm, straight, brisket deep but not barrel-shaped.

Legs and Feet: Forelegs straight and well feathered, hind legs very muscular, hocks strong and well bent. Pads of feet black.

Tail: Very profusely feathered, always held at a downward angle.

Coat: Very long, moderately soft to harsh, flat. Good mane on neck and chest.

Colour: Lion-coloured, golden yellow to russet brown with dark mask.

Height and Weight: Dogs 72—80 cm, bitches 64—74 cm; weight not officially prescribed.

Origin of Breed: Crossing of St. Bernard, Newfoundland and Pyrenean Mountain Dog.

Characteristics and Uses: Quiet, agreeable and affectionate, faithful, good-natured, loves children, reliable, not given to barking and does not look for trouble with other dogs. Reliable watchdog and guard. Needs a good deal of exercise. Excellent swimmer.

Huge imposing dog, used in the past for rescuing the victims of avalanches.

General Appearance: Massive dog, proportionately tall with strong, muscular body, powerful head, dignified and intelligent expression.

Head: Large and massive with broad, slightly rounded skull, flat cheeks and somewhat prominent brow. Stop abrupt and well defined, muzzle short, full in front of eyes and square at nose end. Lips deep but not too pendulous. Nose large and black. Eyes rather small and deep set, not too close together, dark in colour. Ears medium-sized, lying close to the cheeks, not heavily feathered.

Neck: Long, thick, muscular and slightly arched, with well developed dewlap.

Body: Back broad and straight, ribs well rounded, shoulders broad and sloping, chest wide and deep, loin wide and very muscular.

Legs and Feet: Forelegs straight, strongly boned and of good length. Hind legs heavily boned, hocks well bent, thighs muscular.

Tail: Set rather high, long and well feathered in long-haired variety. Carried low in repose, when in action should not be raised over the back.

Coat of Short-haired Variety (above): Should be close and flat, slightly feathered on thighs and tail.

Coat of Long-haired Variety (below): Dense and flat, fuller round the neck, thighs well feathered.

Colour: Orange, mahogany-brindle, red-brindle, white with patches of the above-mentioned colours. Essential markings: white muzzle, white blaze up face, white collar round neck, white chest, white forelegs, feet and end of tail, black shadings on face and ears.

Height and Weight: Dogs at least 75 cm, bitches at least 70 cm; bitches are more slightly built than dogs.

Origin of Breed: St. Bernards appear to be descended from war dogs brought to the Swiss Alps by the Roman legionaries. The monks from the St. Bernard Monastery began to use these dogs for rescuing lost travellers and the victims of avalanches. Later new blood was introduced by crossing with the Newfoundland and Mastiff.

Characteristics and Uses: Good-natured, reliable and quiet, fond of its own home and family but suspicious of strangers. These qualities make it a good watchdog and guard. Unsuitable for small flats and houses.

Spitz   18, 28, 48, 51

Five types of Spitz are recognized: the Wolf Spitz (smoky grey — below), the Great German Spitz (above), the medium, small and toy (Pomeranian). The same standard applies to all, the only difference being in size and colour. Developed in Germany.

General Appearance: Short, square built dog with aggressive stance.

Head: Moderately large, skull widest at the back, tapering towards the nose in a wedge, muzzle not too long. Nose round, small and pure black, or dark brown in the case of brown Spitzes. Eyes medium-sized, dark, rather long and somewhat oblique. Ears small, close together, triangular and pointed, set high and always carried erect.

Neck: Medium length.

Body: Back as short as possible, straight, higher at the front, chest deep, brisket arched, belly slightly drawn in towards the rear.

Legs and Feet: Forelegs moderately long and straight, hind legs rather bent at the hocks. Cat feet.

Tail: Fairly long, set high, carried upwards and forwards right from the root and curled over the back. The tip is curled in a tight circle either to the right or left and lies on the back.

Coat: Profuse, on neck and shoulders looser and standing straight out from the body; should neither wave nor curl, nor be shaggy. Does not form a parting on the back but stands up and then lies flat on the sides of the body. The longest hair is under the neck and on the tail. Legs are feathered.

Colour: **Wolf Spitz**: Smoky or silver grey with dark tips to individual hairs; on muzzle, round the eyes, on the legs, belly and tail the colour is somewhat lighter. **Great German Spitz**: Black, white, brown. **Medium, Small and Toy (Pomeranian) Spitz**: Black, white, orange, smoky grey. The Pomeranian may also come in other colours — blue, cream, beaver and piebald with white as basic colour. Black, brown, grey or orange patches may be scattered over the whole body.

Height and Weight: **Wolf Spitz**: 45—55 cm (up to 60 cm is acceptable if the whole appearance of the dog does not suffer). **Great German Spitz**: 40—50 cm. **Medium Spitz**: 28—36 cm (ideal height 32 cm). **Small Spitz**: 23—28 cm. **Toy (Pomeranian) Spitz**: up to 22 cm (even slightly smaller is acceptable provided the general appearance and health of the dog does not suffer).

Origin of Breed: Breed based on spitz-type dogs found mainly in Pomerania and southern Germany.

Characteristics and Uses: Highly intelligent, sharp, devoted to its master and family but suspicious of strangers. Has all the best watchdog qualities. Coat requires care.

Bulldog 72

The symbol of composure, deliberation, sagacity, tenaciousness and strength. It is often said that the Bulldog is so ugly that is is beautiful. An English breed.

General Appearance: Medium-sized, thickset, smooth-coated dog with strikingly massive head, short wrinkled face and drooping lips.

Head: Skull should be very large, broad, square-shaped, flat between the ears, brow flat and broad, cheeks broad rising up towards the eyes, facial bones very marked and forming a depression between the eyes. Stop very short, muzzle short, broad, deep and turned upwards. Nose large and black. Eyes not too large, dark and wide set. Ears small, thin, rose-shaped, set wide apart and never cropped. Lips thick and overhanging. Undershot.

Neck: Shortish, strong, deep and arched.

Body: Muscular, heavy, back short, broad and roached, chest very wide and capacious, ribs arched, comparatively narrow at loins, belly well tucked up.

Legs and Feet: Forelegs very stout and strong, straight, set wide apart, elbows low, standing well away from the ribs, hind legs strong, longer than forelegs, stifles somewhat turned outward from the body, pasterns short, straight and strong. Feet also slightly turned outwards, round and compact.

Tail: Termed the 'stern' set low, juts out straight and then turns downwards.

Coat: Short, close and smooth, fine and glossy.

Colour: White, tan, pale gold, sandy, brindle and pied.

Height and Weight: Not officially prescribed.

Origin of Breed: Descended from bull baiting dogs of small mastiff type.

Characteristics and Uses: Very intelligent, sagacious, faithful, tough, quiet, good-natured, tenacious, adaptable, sensitive to injustice, does not bark or fight, but would defend its master to the end. Loves children and can adapt itself to them. Ideal pet but not suitable for nervous people. Often there are whelping difficulties.

Dogue de Bordeaux 98

French breed similar to the Mastiff.

General Appearance: Powerful, heavily built, muscular dog, with a short coat, massive head and a long tail carried downwards.

Head: Very capacious, broad and fairly short, stop clearly defined, lips compact, undershot, cheek bulging. Nose broad, black or brown. Eyes large, oval, set wide apart. Ears comparatively small, darker coloured than the rest of the body, held slightly erect and bent forward without being lax.

Neck: Very strong, well muscled, loose skin forming folds.

Body: Back broad, well muscled, withers clearly defined, loin broad, rump slightly downward sloping. Chest powerful, broad, reaching to the elbows.

Legs and Feet: Strongly boned, well muscled, forelegs straight, hind legs angled rather openly, well developed thighs. Feet strong and compact.

Tail: Thick at root, tip not reaching the hocks, in action carried horizontally.

Coat: Short, fine and soft.

Colour: Mahogany to pale fawn, white spots on chest and legs are acceptable. Conspicuous black or red mask.

Height and Weight: Dogs 60—68 cm, bitches 58—66 cm; dogs at least 50 kg, bitches at least 45 kg.

Origin of Breed: Probably descended from original French and Spanish mastiff-type dogs.

Characteristics and Uses: The Dogue de Bordeaux has all the qualities of a good guard dog. It is used as a service and watchdog. At home it is a quiet and good companion but needs a firm hand and a lot of exercise.

Working and utility dog of statuesque build, bred in Germany.

General Appearance: A dog of remarkable size, very muscular, strongly and elegantly built.

Head: Carried high, giving the impression of great length and strength of jaw. The muzzle is broad and the skull proportionately narrow. Face well chiselled. Skull should be flat and have slight indentation up the centre. There should be a rise or brow over the eyes but no abrupt stop between them. Scissors bite. The nose in the case of brindle or self colour dogs is black, in the case of the Harlequins a butterfly or flesh-coloured nose is permitted. Eyes fairly deep set, of moderate size, preferably dark, odd eyes permitted in Harlequins. Ears small, set high on the skull, carried slightly erect with tips falling forward, on the European continent usually cropped to a point.

Neck: Well set on the shoulders, long, well arched, clean and free from loose skin.

Body: The body should be as square as possible, very deep with ribs well sprung and belly well drawn up. Back and loins should be strong.

Legs and Feet: Shoulders strong and muscular, well sloped back, with elbows well under the body. Forelegs straight with big, flat bone. Thighs muscular and second thighs long and well developed. Feet cat-like turning neither in nor out.

Tail: Thick, reaching to or just below the hocks. In action should be carried in a straight line, level with the back.

Coat: Short, dense and sleek-looking.

Colour: Brindles, ground colour from light yellow to deep orange, must be striped, the stripes always being black. In fawns, the colour varies from light buff to deep orange, darker shades on muzzle and ears and around eyes are acceptable. In blues, the colour varies from light grey to deep slate. In blacks the black is black. The nose is always black except in blues. Harlequins have pure white underground with preferably black patches.

Height and Weight: Dogs at least 80 cm, bitches at least 72 cm; weight in proportion to height (50—80 kg).

Origin of Breed: Descended from large mastiff-type dogs kept in Ancient Times as war dogs and for hunting. Probably crossed with such dissimilar breeds as the Greyhound.

Characteristics and Uses: The Great Dane is good-natured and affectionate to its family, especially to children, but is reserved and suspicious of strangers. It is not true that Great Danes become ill-tempered with advancing age. Bad individuals are the result of a bad environment and bad handling. The Great Dane is an excellent watchdog and guard, but can also be trained as a service dog. Needs a great deal of exercise and plenty of food. Unsuitable for a small flat or house.

Mastiff 120

One of the largest and quite the heaviest of dogs. An English breed.

General Appearance: Large, powerful, symmetrical short-haired dog, with massive square head, blunt muzzle, massive deep body, button ears and long tail.

Head: Skull broad between the ears, forehead flat but wrinkled when excited. Clearly defined but not too sharp stop, muscles of temples and cheeks well developed, muzzle short, broad under the eyes. Lips slightly pendulous, scissors bite or slightly undershot. Nose broad, flat, with wide nostrils. Eyes small and wide apart, dark hazel. Small thin ears set wide apart and lying flat when in repose.

Neck: Moderately long, slightly arched, very muscular.

Body: Back and loins wide and muscular, ribs arched and well rounded. Chest wide, deep and well let down.

Legs and Feet: Legs straight, strong and set wide apart. Broad, wide and muscular hind quarters with well developed second thighs. Feet large and round, toes well arched.

Tail: Wide at root, tapering to the end, hanging straight in repose.

Coat: Short and close lying, but not too fine over the shoulders, neck and back.

Colour: Apricot or silver, fawn or dark fawn-brindle. Muzzle, ears and nose black.

Height and Weight: Dogs at least 76 cm, bitches at least 69 cm; weight proportionate (75—90 kg).

Origin of Breed: Probably descended from the Molossian war dogs of Ancient Times.

Characteristics and Uses: A combination of grandeur and good nature, courage and docility. Peace-loving, well mannered, affectionate to members of its master's family, but a fierce defender of its home. Good house dog and watchdog. Needs a great deal of exercise.

Hovawart 103

German breed of working dog whose name is derived from the words Hof and Warte.

General Appearance: Moderately large, strong but not clumsy, long-haired dog with drop ears and a long tail.

Head: Powerful, brow domed and broad, bridge of nose straight and not too long, lips lying flat, scissors bite. Nose well developed. Eyes dark, medium-sized. Triangular drop ears.

Neck: Moderately long, well covered with hair, no dewlap.

Body: Back firm, straight, brisket broad, deep and strong, rump slightly sloping and not too long. Length of the body should be greater than height at the shoulder.

Legs and Feet: Strong and straight, forelegs well covered with hair, shoulder blades slanting, long, hind legs well bent and well muscled. Hocks strong. Feet compact.

Tail: Long, well covered with hair, reaches to below the hocks, in action carried high.

Coat: Long, slightly wavy but never curly.

Colour: Fawn, black, black with brown markings.

Height and Weight: Dogs 63—70 cm, bitches 55—65 cm; weight not officially prescribed.

Origin of Breed: Descended from watchdogs from the Harz Mountains and the Black Forest.

Characteristics and Uses: Intelligent, noble, wary, faithful, good-natured, fond of children but can be fierce when necessary. Good guard dog. Needs plenty of exercise.

Mastino Napoletano (Neapolitan Mastiff) 115

Italian dog of mastiff type, somewhat similar to the Dogue de Bordeaux.

General Appearance: Powerful, heavy, majestic dog whose very appearance inspires respect.

Head: Massive, skull broad, short and flat, muzzle blunt, stop clearly defined. Jaws very strong, scissors bite, lips thick, upper covering lower. Eyes oval. Ears comparatively small, triangular, carried erect from the roots but with ends dropped.

Neck: Short, thickset with excessive loose skin forming a dewlap.

Body: Back level and broad, chest deep and rather arched, belly capacious, lightly tucked up.

Legs and Feet: Straight, strong and well muscled, hind legs broad-thighed and well-angled. Feet compact, toes closed up.

Tail: Thick at root, tapering towards the tip, docked if long.

Coat: Short and close-lying.

Colour: Most often black, leaden, grey, roan, tan.

Height and Weight: Dogs 65—75 cm, bitches 60—70 cm; weight not officially prescribed.

Origin of Breed: Probably descended from the ancient war dogs of the Roman Legions.

Characteristics and Uses: Quiet, very affectionate, intelligent, fearless, rather suspicious of strangers. Perfect watchdog and guard. Needs a firm hand.

Samoyed 70

'The dog with a smiling face' is the epithet often applied to this northern spitz of Russian origin.

General Appearance: Medium-sized, long-haired, fine looking dog with small prick ears and a profusely coated tail.

Head: Powerful, wedge-shaped with a broad, flat skull, muzzle of medium size and a tapering foreface though not too pointed, scissors bite. Nose black or brown. Eyes almond-shaped, medium to dark brown, set well apart giving the dog its typical smile. Ears small, slightly rounded at the tips, held erect.

Neck: Medium in length, well arched with profuse hair.

Body: Back medium in length, broad and very muscular. Chest broad, deep and roomy.

Legs and Feet: Forelegs straight and muscular, hind legs very muscular, stifles well angulated. Feet long, flattish and slightly spread out. Profuse hair between the toes.

Tail: Long and profusely covered, carried over the back when alert, sometimes dropped when in repose.

Coat: Thick, short, soft undercoat with harsh hair growing through it to form outercoat standing straight away from the body.

Colour: Pure white, white and biscuit, cream.

Height and Weight: Dogs 52—55 cm, bitches from 45.5 cm; dogs 22—30 kg, bitches 17—25 kg.

Origin of Breed: One of the Spitz group, a type of dog which evolved very early in man's history.

Characteristics and Uses: Intelligent, alert, faithful and very affectionate dog, particularly fond of children. Is a good draught and guard dog and likes to have plenty of work.

Styrian Bracke   53

Austrian sporting dog which can work well in mountains or lowlands.
General Appearance: Moderately large, well muscled dog.
Head: Medium-sized, slightly domed, occipital crest well developed. Slight break between muzzle and forehead. Nose black. Length of head from occipital crest to the tip of the nose 22—24 cm. Eyes clear, usually brown to golden yellow, wise expression. Ears not too large, hanging smoothly close to the head, covered with smoother and softer hair than the rest of the body.
Neck: Strong, not too long, carried in a rather upward curve.
Body: Back broad, length from occipital crest to root of tail 65—70 cm. Brisket deep, 66—79 cm in circumference. Belly slightly tucked up.
Legs and Feet: Legs straight and muscular, pads not very large, toes compact.
Tail: Moderately long, thick at the root, well covered with hair which forms a brush on the underside, carried up in a slightly sickle-like curve.
Coat: Very slightly wavy, almost without gloss, harsh and rough to the touch. Chest and rear side of forelegs slightly feathered.
Colour: Blackish and fawny yellow, white blaze on the chest is acceptable, other white markings not permissible.
Height and Weight: 40—50 cm; weight not officially prescribed.
Origin of Breed: Result of crossing Hannoverian Bloodhound with Istrian Schweisshund.
Characteristics and Uses: Comparatively quiet and amenable, with an excellent nose. Highly suitable for hunting wild boar. Very faithful family companion.

Slovak Kopov (Lurcher)   61

The only hound-type breed developed in Czechoslovakia.
General Appearance: Lightly built body, firm frame, self coloured or black and tan, square-shaped.
Head: Muzzle straight, not too wide, lips shortish and not overhanging, stop at an angle of around 45°. Eyes deep set, dark. Ears set a little above the level of the eyes, close-lying, moderately long.
Neck: Well set on, carried at an angle of about 135°.
Body: Chest broad and well filled, brisket moderately deep, back straight of medium length, belly and flanks slightly tucked up, rump shortish and rounded.
Legs and Feet: Shoulders and forequarters rather shorter, well developed and muscular. Thighs broad, proportionately long, muscular. Feet oval, toes well closed in, arched forwards.
Tail: Fairly strong, set below the level of the back.
Coat: 2—5 cm long, fairly rough, flat and dense, rather longer on back, neck and tail.
Colour: Self colour, black and tan.
Height and Weight: Dogs 45—50 cm, bitches 40—45 cm; 15—20 kg.
Origin of Breed: Descended from watchdogs also used for hunting.
Characteristics and Uses: Very persistent and enthusiastic to give tongue when following a warm scent, sharp, amenable to its own family. Can quickly learn to track by scent. Needs a firm hand.

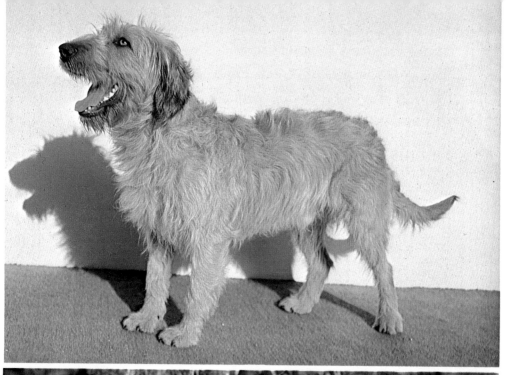

Dogo Argentino (Argentinian Hound)   87

Dog used for hunting big game in the Argentinian pampas.

General Appearance: Large well proportioned dog with a white coat, pricked or semi-pricked ears and long tail carried downwards.

Head: Similar to that of the Great Dane, skull domed, muzzle same length as skull, jaws strong, neither overshot nor undershot, lips well rounded, taut and with black pigmentation. Nose also has black pigmentation. Eyes dark or hazel. Ears carried high, often cropped, erect or semi-erect.

Neck: Strong, arched and slender, with wrinkles on throat.

Body: Back straight, strong and well muscled, line of back falling slightly towards the rump.

Legs and Feet: Forelegs straight and vertical, very muscular thighs, dewclaws on hind legs. Toes short, well closed with hard skin.

Tail: Long and thick, in action held high and waving from side to side.

Coat: Short and dense.

Colour: Pure white. Any coloured markings are reason for disqualification.

Height and Weight: Dogs about 60 cm, bitches about 58 cm; dogs 45 kg, bitches 35 kg.

Origin of Breed: Amongst the ancestors of this breed were the large mastiff-type dogs which reached South America with the Spanish colonizers.

Characteristics and Uses: Strong, quick and persevering. Reliable hound and retriever. Has also proved a good service dog.

Basenji   49

An African hunting dog of very ancient origin. Does not bark though it is able to make a chortling sound. Its indigenous owners sometimes hang a bell round its neck so that they can follow when it is tracking game.

General Appearance: Lightly built, finely boned, alert dog occurring in two varieties: the plainland or White Basenji is lighter in colour while the 'forest type' is darker.

Head: Skull flat, well chiselled, of medium width. Muzzle tapers towards the nose with only a slight stop. Fine and profuse wrinkles on the forehead when the ears are pricked, giving the dog its characteristic worried expression. Eyes, almond-shaped, obliquely set, usually dark but can be yellow or even pale blue in lighter varieties. Ears small, pointed, erect and slightly hooded, set well forward.

Neck: Strong and of good length, well crested and slightly full at base of throat.

Body: Balanced with short, level back. Ribs well sprung, deep and oval. The loin short-coupled and the brisket deep, running up to a definite waist.

Legs and Feet: Forelegs straight, fine boned, with long forearms. Hind legs strong and muscular with long second thighs. Feet small, narrow and compact.

Tail: Set high, curled tightly over the spine.

Coat: Short, sleek and close.

Colour: In plainland type light beige with white shirtfront. Forest type pure bright red, or pure black or black and tan, all with white feet, chest and tail tip.

Height and Weight: Dogs about 43 cm, bitches about 40 cm; dogs about 10.8 kg, bitches about 9.9 kg.

Origin of Breed: An original Congolese breed.

Characteristics and Uses: Intelligent, lively, obedient, playful and exceptionally clean, with very good hunting qualities. Used for starting game in its native land.

Basset Artesian Normand   25

Best known of French Basset Hounds.
General Appearance: Short-legged, powerful, short-haired dog with elongated body, long drooping ears and a fairly long tail.
Head: Domed, lean and slightly wrinkled appearance. Stop well defined, occipital crest very striking, bridge of nose moderately long, rather broad, slightly arched, scissors bite. Nose black. Eyes large and dark. Ears very long, set low.
Neck: Rather long with small dewlap.
Body: Broad, long, loins slightly arched, flanks drooping, chest broad, breastbone clearly projecting.
Legs and Feet: Forelegs short, powerful and slightly crooked, shoulders short, strong and well muscled. Hind thighs very fleshy and muscular, hip joints slightly slanting, hocks slightly bent and strong. Feet large, all toes touching the ground.
Tail: Long, sometimes curving upwards but not curling onto the back.
Coat: Short, smooth, flat, not too fine.
Colour: Tricolour or bicolour (white and orange).
Height and Weight: 26—36 cm; weight not officially prescribed (about 15 kg).
Origin of Breed: Result of crossing original French breeds.
Characteristics and Uses: Intelligent, gentle, serious, very devoted, amenable, tolerant. Excellent sporting hound and very agreeable companion. Needs plenty of exercise.

Basset Fauve de Bretagne   31

Well-tried French short-haired hound.
General Appearance: Short-legged dog with long, strongly built body and drooping ears.
Head: Skull moderately long, occipital crest well defined, muzzle straight or slightly curved, a little elongated. Eyes small with lively expression. Ears fine, moderately long, set at the level of the eyes. Nose black or very dark, nostrils well opened.
Neck: Fairly short, muscular.
Body: Chest broad and deep, back long but not as long as that of other bassets, loins broad and muscular, flanks full, hip joints well defined.
Legs and Feet: Short and strong, shoulders strong, somewhat sloping, thighs muscular. Feet lean, close and compact.
Tail: Stern thick at root, not over long, carried like a sickle, tapering towards the tip.
Coat: Very harsh, thick, rather short, lying close to the body.
Colour: Light beige, sometimes with white fleck on the chest.
Height and Weight: 32—36 cm; weight not officially prescribed.
Origin of Breed: Old French breed originating in Brittany.
Characteristics and Uses: Stout-hearted hound with an exceptionally sensitive nose and inborn talent for tracking. An affectionate and gentle dog. Fond of children.

Basset Hound   37

American breed of short-legged hound of similar build to the Dachshund.

General Appearance: Long-bodied, short-legged hound of considerable substance with free action.

Head: Domed, with some stop and prominent occipital bone, of medium width at the brow and tapering slightly to the muzzle. There may be a moderate amount of wrinkle at the brows and beside the eyes. Nose dark with well opened nostrils. Eyes brown, may shade to hazel in light-coloured hounds, expression serious. Ears set low, very long, very supple, fine and velvety.

Neck: Muscular and fairly long, with pronounced dewlap.

Body: Back long, broad, level. Breastbone slightly prominent, chest not too narrow or unduly deep.

Legs and Feet: Shoulder blades well laid back, forelegs short, powerful and with great bone, elbows turned neither in nor out but fitting against the side. Hind legs muscular, hocks close to the ground not turned in nor out. Feet massive.

Tail: Long, well set on, strong at base and tapering. In action stern is carried well up and curves gently, sabre fashion over the back.

Coat: Smooth, short and close without being too fine. Skin loose and supple.

Colour: Any recognized hound colour.

Height and Weight: Height should not exceed 38 cm; weight proportionate (about 23 kg).

Origin of Breed: Result of crossing the Basset Artesian Normand with the Bloodhound.

Characteristics and Uses: Serious, with gentle temperament, neither too lively nor too shy. Not clumsy, very hardy and exceptionally devoted. While a reliable sporting dog it is today mostly kept as a house dog. Needs plenty of exercise.

Beagle   35

Small lively hound, used in Great Britain for hunting hare but is more often kept as a pet.

General Appearance: Sturdy, compactly built hound, conveying the impression of quality without coarseness.

Head: Fair length, skull slightly domed, moderately wide with indication of peak. Stop well defined, muzzle not pointed, lips reasonably well flewed. Nose broad, preferably black. Eyes brown or hazel, fairly large, set well apart. Ears long with round tip, set low, fine in texture, hanging close to the cheeks, finely coated.

Neck: Fairly long, slightly arched, with a little dewlap.

Body: Topline straight and level. Chest well let down to below elbow. Ribs well sprung. Loins powerful.

Legs and Feet: Forelegs straight and upright, strong, hard and round in bone. Muscular thighs. Stifles well bent. Feet tight and firm, well knuckled up.

Tail: Sturdy and of moderate length. Set high and carried gaily but not curled over the back.

Coat: In smooth-haired variety dense, not too short and fine, in rough-haired dogs very dense and wiry.

Colour: Any recognized hound colour other than liver. Tip of stern white.

Height and Weight: 33—38 cm; weight proportionate (about 17 kg).

Origin of Breed: Small hounds like Beagles have been known since the sixteenth century if not earlier.

Characteristics and Uses: A lively smart little hound with a self-confident air. Needs plenty of exercise and enjoys using its nose.

One of the oldest breeds of German hunting dog to survive to the present day.
General Appearance: Short-legged, powerfully built, long-bodied dog with fairly long ears and a long tail.
Head: Moderately large, wider at the brow than at the cheeks, stop barely perceptible, bridge of the nose slightly arched. Nose dark or light according to the colour of the coat, lips somewhat overhanging, scissors bite. Eyes dark and large. Ears moderately long, broad, rounded at the tips, flat against the head.
Neck: Fairly long and thick, loose skin forming no dewlap.
Body: Back moderately long, slightly lowered beyond the shoulders, hind quarters broad and strong, rump descending slantwise, chest narrow and not too deep, brisket long, belly slightly tucked up.
Legs and Feet: Forelegs strongly boned and sinewy, straight when viewed from the front, elbows flat to the body, hind legs more sturdy than in other dogs, thighs strong, well muscled, feet compact.
Tail: Set comparatively high, carried horizontally, hair on lower side forming a brush.
Coat: Very dense and rough, short on head, ears and lower part of legs, longer on back, neck and underside of body.
Colour: Any colour other than black or chocolate brown.
Height and Weight: 30—35 cm; weight not officially prescribed.
Origin of Breed: Descended from original breed.
Characteristics and Uses: Easy to manage, persistent, excellent at seeking and following a scent, an exceptional grasp of locality. Should be owned solely by sportsmen.

Irish Water Spaniel   71

A type of gundog bred for work in all types of shooting and particularly for wild-fowling.
General Appearance: Muscular moderately large dog, differing from other breeds of Spaniel in its unusual coat and gait.
Head: Of good size with high, domed skull. Muzzle long, strong and somewhat square with a gradual stop. Nose large and well developed, dark liver colour. Scissors bite. Eyes comparatively small and alert. Ears very long, lobe-shaped, set low, hanging close to the cheeks.
Neck: Powerful, long, carrying the head well above the level of the back.
Body: Short, broad and level back, loins deep and wide. Chest deep and of large girth.
Legs and Feet: Forelegs well boned and straight, with arms well let down. Hind legs powerful with well bent stifles and hocks set low. Feet large, round and spreading.
Tail: Short, straight, thick at root and tapering to a fine point, not docked.
Coat: Composed of dense, tight, crisp ringlets free from woolliness, naturally oily. Skull covered with long curls in the form of a pronounced topknot growing to a peak between the eyes, long twisted curls covering the ears. Forelegs covered with feather in curls or ringlets down to the feet. About 8—10 cm of the tail at the root covered in close curls which stop abruptly, the remainder being bare or covered with straight fine hair.
Colour: Rich dark liver with purplish tint sometimes referred to as puce liver.
Height and Weight: Dogs 53—58 cm, bitches 51—56 cm; weight in proportion to height.
Origin of Breed: Old Irish breed, said to be the result of crossing the Spaniel and Poodle.
Characteristics and Uses: Intelligent, enduring and eager. Suitable for all types of shooting, especially work in water. Also makes an agreeable family dog.

Cocker Spaniel   47

One of the oldest original English breeds of gundog. Its name is derived from the word 'woodcock'.

General Appearance: Medium-sized, long-haired, very active merry dog.

Head: Nicely developed, square muzzle, skull straight with distinct stop, cleanly chiselled. Skull and occiput well developed. Nose fairly wide. Eyes full, round, hazel or brown in colour. Ears lobular, set low, fine, covered with long silky hair.

Neck: Long, muscular, neatly set on to fine sloping shoulders.

Body: Compact and firmly knit. Short, unusually strong and firm back, slightly slanting towards the tail.

Legs and Feet: Forelegs straight and well boned, appropriately feathered and sufficiently short for concentrated power. Hind legs set broad, very muscular, well feathered, straight, short enough for concentrated power. Feet firm, round, cat-like.

Tail: Set low, never held upright, should not be docked too short. When working the tail is always in movement and this is a characteristic feature of a well bred Spaniel.

Coat: Flat and silky in texture, never wiry and rough, with sufficient feather but must not be too profuse and never curly.

Colour: Can vary considerably. In self-coloured individuals there can be a white blaze on the chest.

Height and Weight: Dogs 39—41 cm, bitches 38—39 cm; 12—14.5 kg.

Origin of Breed: Descended from the type of sporting dogs used in England for flushing small game from cover.

Characteristics and Uses: The Cocker Spaniel is now mainly kept as a pet for which its desire to please and its affectionate nature make it eminently suitable. The wide range of coat colour and the breed's friendliness have been the main factors in its popularity. The coat and ears require considerable care and the breed tends to put on weight unless well exercised and sensibly fed. Though it retains its sporting instincts, few Cocker Spaniels now work with the gun. As well as a shy or vicious temperament, faults include a coarse skull, light bone, curly coat, straight shoulders, poor movement, weak hocks, high tail carriage, deficient stop, light eyes.

American Cocker Spaniel   40

Differs from the Cocker Spaniel in being more thickset with a shorter, more domed head and profuse coat. A North American breed.

General Appearance: Dog with robust compact body with moderately long coat, lobular ears and docked tail.

Head: Skull rounded, projecting brow and distinct stop, muzzle wide and deep with square jaw, upper lips deep enough to cover lower jaw, scissors bite. Eyes slightly almond-shaped, hazel or dark brown to black in colour. Ears long, set low, well feathered.

Neck: Fairly long, muscular, no throatiness.

Body: Back robust, brisket deep, chest fairly wide but not so wide as to restrict movement of forelegs, hips broad, rump muscular.

Legs and Feet: Forelegs straight, parallel, muscular and well boned. Hind legs also well boned and well angled, hocks strong. Feet round turning neither out nor in.

Tail: Docked and carried on a level with the back or slightly higher, when in action in constant movement.

Coat: Silky in texture, straight or slightly wavy, on head short, on body moderately long, on ears, chest, flanks and legs forming fringes.

Colour: All coal black, self colour in other shades, black and tan.

Height and Weight: Dogs 38—40 cm, bitches rather less; weight not officially prescribed.

Origin of Breed: Descended from original breeds of Spaniel.

Characteristics and Uses: Intelligent, reliable, amenable, good looking, amiable, devoted, merry even temperament, not shy or nervous, able to develop considerable speed combined with great powers of endurance. Coat requires a certain amount of care. Rarely used as a gundog but very popular as a pet.

Springer Spaniel 66

The oldest of English sporting gundogs.

General Appearance: Medium-sized, strong, self-confident, lively and hard working dog, built for endurance and efficiency.

Head: Skull moderately long, comparatively broad, slightly rounded. Occipital crest neither peaked nor very apparent, cheeks flat, muzzle comparatively wide and deep, square-shaped. Eyes hazel. Ears lobular, lying flat to the head.

Neck: Strong, muscular, moderately long and nicely arched.

Body: Strong and of proportionate length, chest deep, well sprung ribs, loins strong, muscular, slightly arched.

Legs and Feet: Forelegs straight, well feathered, hind legs well let down from hips to hocks, feet compact.

Tail: Set low, well feathered with lively action, docked.

Coat: Smooth-lying and straight, weather-resistant but never harsh.

Colour: Liver and white, black and white or one or other with tan markings preferred.

Height and Weight: 50—52 cm; about 22.5 kg.

Origin of Breed: Descended from the same ancestors as the Cocker Spaniel. When spaniels began to be distinguished according to weight, the Springer Spaniel was the type weighing 25 lb or over.

Characteristics and Uses: The Springer Spaniel is popular as a rough shooter's dog being used to find, flush and retrieve for the gun any type of small game up to the size of a hare. They are one of the larger spaniels and, being active, robust dogs, they need plenty of exercise and training when kept solely as pets.

Welsh Springer Spaniel 62

Among the most beautiful of the spaniels.

General Appearance: Symmetrical, compact, strong, merry and very active dog. Built for endurance and hard work.

Head: Skull moderately long, a little arched with clearly defined stop. Muzzle of medium length, straight, fairly square. Eyes hazel or dark, medium-sized, ears comparatively small, narrowing gradually to the tip, covered with light feathering.

Neck: Long, muscular, clean in throat.

Body: Not long, strong, muscular with deep brisket.

Legs and Feet: Forelegs of medium length, straight and well boned, lightly feathered. Hind legs also moderately feathered, strong and muscular with deep second thighs, hocks well let down, stifles moderately bent. Feet round with thick pads.

Tail: Well set on and low, never carried above the level of the back. Slightly covered and lively in action. Docked.

Coat: Straight or flat and thick, silky texture, never wiry or wavy.

Colour: Dark rich red and white only.

Height and Weight: Dogs about 48 cm, bitches about 45 cm; weight not officially prescribed.

Origin of Breed: Improved from original English breeds.

Characteristics and Uses: Exceptionally well developed talent for hunting, tireless, affectionate, fast and very willing to work. The Welsh Springer Spaniel needs consistent obedience training as it is inclined to be self-willed.

Wachtelhund (German Spaniel) 67

The sole continental breed for flushing game.
General Appearance: Similar to that of the German Long-haired Pointer.
Head: Lean, with thin lips. Muzzle long, stop scarcely perceptible. Eyes dark brown, viewed from the side they appear to be set obliquely. Ears set high and wide apart, carried pendent close to the head. Nose brown and as large as possible.
Neck: Strong, fine and without dewlap.
Body: Length of back line greater than height at the shoulder. Back short and level, brisket reaches to the elbows.
Legs and Feet: Outer line of forelegs and feet vertical. Rump long, thighs widely set, hocks very strong. Hind legs should be well angled and not set under the body.
Tail: Set high, well coated with hair, in repose carried horizontally or downwards, docked.
Coat: Strong, dense, wavy, long. On neck and ears is often curly.
Colour: Dark brown with white markings on chest and toes, roan, white, tricolour.
Height and Weight: Dogs 45—52 cm, bitches 40—45 cm; weight not officially prescribed.
Origin of Breed: Bred from original German gundog.
Characteristics and Uses: Persevering, all-round gundog for work in forest and in water. Typical tracker, gives tongue when it finds a scent. Needs good training and a firm hand. Coat requires no special care.

Bavarian Gebirgsschweisshund 65

Younger and smaller brother of the Hannover Schweisshund. A German breed.
General Appearance: Very active medium-sized dog.
Head: Upper part rather wide, skull domed, break between eyes and muzzle. Eyes dark brown or slightly lighter. Ears heavy and pendent, rounded at the tips.
Neck: Moderately long, strong and slim.
Body: Back very strong, hind quarters broad, deep and well muscled as far as the flanks, always slightly arched. Brisket deep, belly slightly tucked up.
Legs and Feet: Forelegs viewed from the front completely straight, well muscled, thighs very broad and long, pastern placed vertically to the ground. Feet spoon-shaped, well coated with hair.
Tail: Moderately long, carried horizontally or slightly downwards.
Coat: Dense, flat and slightly wiry.
Colour: Dark red, deer red, red-brown, red-yellow, ochre, pale yellow to wheaten, grey-brown, tan, dark brindle.
Height and Weight: Dogs under 50 cm, bitches under 45 cm; weight not officially prescribed.
Origin of Breed: By crossing light Alpine Bracke with Hannover Schweisshund.
Characteristics and Uses: More agile and persistent in high mountainous terrain than the Hannover Schweisshund. Unequalled at scenting out wounded game. No special care required for this breed.

Hannover Schweisshund 77

German breed which specializes in seeking out wounded game including wild boar.

General Appearance: Moderately large dog of elongated build.

Head: Medium-sized, broad, slightly domed, rather narrower at the front than at the back. Brow slightly wrinkled, occipital crest not very marked. Nose black, brown or red. Eyes clear. Ears rather long, very broad.

Neck: Long and strong, no dewlap.

Body: Back long, loins broad and slightly arched, rump falling obliquely. Brisket broad, deep and long.

Legs and Feet: Forelegs thicker than hind legs, shoulder blades loose and mobile, thighs muscular, second thighs long. Feet round.

Tail: Long, reaching at least to the middle of the hock.

Coat: Dense, smooth and pliant.

Colour: Greyish brown, red-brown, red-yellow, ochre, dark yellow or brown with dark flecks or brindle, a dark stripe running down the back.

Height and Weight: Dogs 50—55 cm, bitches 48—53 cm; weight not officially prescribed.

Origin of Breed: Descendant of various breeds used to follow the scent of blood.

Characteristics and Uses: Quiet, serious, persistent sporting dog, with a passion for hunting and an unusually sensitive nose. Can track a scent over long distances even under very unfavourable weather conditions. Requires long and patient training.

Bloodhound 111

The word 'blood' in this hound's name does not indicate that it is bloodthirsty but that it hunts by scent. The Bloodhound is, in fact, a very quiet, gentle and peace-loving dog of English breed.

General Appearance: Large, strong, short-haired dog with noble and dignified expression, characterized by its solemnity, wisdom and power which results from the extremely loose skin hanging in deep folds around the head.

Head: Head is narrow in proportion to its length and long in proportion to the body, tapering only slightly from temples to square-shaped muzzle. Eyes deeply sunk varying from deep hazel to yellow. Ears thin and soft, extremely long, set low, falling in graceful folds. Lips fall squarely forming deep hanging flews. Scissors bite.

Neck: Long, powerful, well developed dewlap.

Body: Back and loins strong. Ribs well sprung, chest well let down between the forelegs forming a deep keel.

Legs and Feet: Shoulders muscular, well set backwards. Forelegs straight, large and round in bone with elbows squarely set. Thighs and second thighs very muscular. Feet strong and well knuckled up.

Tail: Stern is long and thick, tapering to a point, set high with moderate amount of hair underneath. Carried scimitar fashion.

Coat: On body harsh, on head and ears soft.

Colour: Black and tan, liver and tan (red and tan), and red. A small amount of white permissible on chest, feet and tip of stern.

Height and Weight: Dogs about 67 cm, bitches about 60 cm; 40—48 kg.

Origin of Breed: Probably derived from the Black Bracke or Braque from St. Hubert's Monastery in the Ardennes.

Characteristics and Uses: Dignified, quiet dog, not in the least quarrelsome or aggressive. Very sensitive to praise or reprimands. Utterly devoted to its master, rather reserved and aloof with strangers. Has unbelievably sensitive nose. Rather difficult to breed as the puppies are often delicate.

Pointer 105

Sole type of English short-haired pointing dog.
General Appearance: Graceful, symmetrical, well built short-coated dog.
Head: Skull of medium length in proportion to length of foreface, stop well defined, pronounced occipital bone. Muzzle somewhat concave. Eyes either hazel or brown. Ears set rather high, drooping close to the head.
Neck: Long, muscular, slightly arched, springing cleanly from shoulders.
Body: Brisket well let down, well sprung ribs, couplings short.
Legs and Feet: Forelegs straight and firm. Knee joint flat with front of leg. Thighs large, very muscular as are second thighs. Feet oval, with well knit, arched toes.
Tail: Of medium length, thick at root, growing gradually thinner to the point. Carried on a level with the back.
Coat: Fine, short, hard, smooth and straight.
Colour: Lemon and white, orange and white, liver and white, black and white. Self-colours and tricolours are also correct.
Height and Weight: Dogs 63—68 cm, bitches 61—66 cm; weight not officially prescribed.
Origin of Breed: According to some it originally came from Spain; others affirm that the Pointer is an original English breed.
Characteristics and Uses: Has an exceptionally sensitive nose, can find a scent from a great distance and react with lightening speed. Lively, hardworking and biddable. Not particularly difficult to breed.

English Setter 108

A gundog of truly stately appearance.
General Appearance: Above medium size, long coat, graceful lines.
Head: Skull long, oval from ear to ear, with well defined occipital crest, muzzle fairly square. Eyes hazel. Ears of moderate length, set low, hanging in neat folds close to the cheeks.
Neck: Rather long, muscular, lean, not throaty.
Body: Back of moderate length, level. Chest should be deep in the brisket, wide between the shoulder blades and well arched.
Legs and Feet: Shoulders should be well set back or oblique, long forearm very muscular, elbow well let down. Loins should be broad, well arched, thighs strong, long from hip to hock. Feet very close and compact.
Tail: Medium length, slightly curved or scimitar-shaped.
Coat: Slightly wavy, long and silky. Breeches and forelegs down to the feet should be well feathered as should be the tail.
Colour: Black and white, lemon and white, liver and white, black with white and tan.
Height and Weight: Dogs 64—68 cm, bitches 61—65 cm; dogs 27—29.5 kg, bitches 25—28 kg.
Origin of Breed: Bred from original long-haired English Pointer.
Characteristics and Uses: Very devoted to its own family. Coat requires a fair amount of attention. A very elegant, beautiful dog whose amenable disposition makes it popular choice with pet owners. Now far better known in the show ring and the home than in the field, but, like all the setters, needs plenty of exercise.

The rarest of the setters, now known mainly in the show ring.

General Appearance: Stylish dog, of large build particularly constructed for speed, perfectly proportioned.

Head: Rather deeper than wide. Eyes dark brown. Ears pendent, set low and lying close to the head.

Neck: Long, lean, arched towards the head, with no dewlap.

Body: Brisket deep, shoulders broad and slightly arched, chest not too broad.

Legs and Feet: Forelegs long with oval bones and firm straight pasterns. Hind legs long from hip to hock, broad and muscular. Feet round with sufficient hair between the toes.

Tail: Comparatively short, straight or slightly scimitar-shaped, carried horizontally or slightly below the level of the back. The feathering on the tail is long and straight.

Coat: On head, front of legs and tips of ears short and fine, on other parts of the body long and straight.

Colour: Black with tan markings.

Height and Weight: Dogs about 66 cm, bitches about 62 cm; dogs 29 kg, bitches 25 kg.

Origin of Breed: Bred and improved from original Scottish setter.

Characteristics and Uses: Quiet, amenable dog of a rather heavier type but extremely elegant and graceful. Can be used for any work with guns appropriate to setters and pointers, scenting in fields and woods and particularly suited for work in water. Easy to breed. It is a satisfactory pet and house dog.

Irish Setter 95

An elegant, racy dog, kept mainly as a show dog and companion.

General Appearance: Above average size, elegant, racy dog, gentle in expression.

Head: Long, well defined occipital crest, muzzle fairly deep, almost square at end. Eyes hazel or dark brown. Ears not too large, set low and well back, hanging in neat folds close to the head.

Neck: Moderately long, very muscular but not too thick, slightly arched.

Body: Proportionate with well sprung ribs.

Legs and Feet: Forelegs straight and sinewy, elbows free, well let down. Hind legs wide, from hip to hock long and muscular. Feet small, firm and compact.

Tail: Moderately long, set rather low, strong at root then tapering, carried as near as possible level with the back or slightly below.

Coat: On head, front of the legs and tips of the ears short and fine. On all other parts of the body and legs of moderate length and flat. On the upper part of the ears long and silky. On the back of the legs long and fine. Feet well feathered.

Colour: Rich chestnut with no trace of black.

Height and Weight: Dogs 61—65 cm, bitches 56—61 cm; weight not officially prescribed (25—30 kg).

Origin of Breed: By selection of red dogs from red and white setters.

Characteristics and Uses: A stylish, racy, headstrong dog with a loving disposition. Needs plenty of exercise and its beautiful colouring can best be appreciated when it is galloping freely. Very little used in the field anymore.

Hungarian Vizsla (Short-haired) 83

Elegant, hardworking gundog, very keen, of Hungarian origin.

General Appearance: Medium-sized dog of distinguished appearance, robust but not too heavily boned.

Head: Skull moderately wide between the ears with a median line down the forehead and a moderate stop. Muzzle should be a little longer than the skull and although tapering should be well squared at the end. Eyes slightly oval in shape. Ears moderately low set and hanging close to the cheeks, rounded U-shaped. Large, rounded nose.

Neck: Moderately long, held fairly high.

Body: Back should be level, short, well muscled, withers high. Chest moderately deep. Ribs well sprung, belly tight with slight tuck-up beneath the loin.

Legs and Feet: Shoulders well laid and muscular, elbows straight, pointing neither in nor out. Hind legs straight when viewed from the rear, thighs well developed. Feet rounded with short toes.

Tail: Rather low set, with one third docked off. Whilst moving should be held horizontally.

Coat: Should be short and straight, dense, glossy and feel greasy to the touch.

Colour: Russet gold.

Height and Weight: Dogs 57—64 cm, bitches 53—60 cm; weight proportionate (22—30 kg).

Origin of Breed: Result of crossing the Pointer with the Schweisshund and possibly other breeds of gundog.

Characteristics and Uses: Intelligent, obedient, affectionate and easily trained. Good for hunting fur and feather, pointing and retrieving from both land and water. Sensitive to harsh treatment.

Hungarian Vizsla (Wire-haired) 84

Rough-coated edition of the short-haired Hungarian Vizsla.

General Appearance: Moderate-sized type of pointer of pleasing appearance with well balanced, strong but not coarse muscles.

Head, Neck, Body, Legs and Feet, Tail: The same as in short-haired variety.

Coat: Rough, lying close to the body, without gloss. Forms whiskers on the chin. On ears rather longer and finer. On neck and body about 3—4 cm long.

Colour: Russet gold.

Height and Weight: Dogs 57—64 cm, bitches 53—60 cm; 22—30 kg.

Origin of Breed: Bred from Hungarian Short-haired Vizsla with an admixture of German Wire-haired Pointer blood. Sometimes a litter includes short-haired pups and pups differing in colour from the standard.

Characteristics and Uses: The same as for the Short-haired Vizsla. Particularly adapted to work in water.

German Short-haired Pointer   90

Most widespread breed of short-haired pointer on the continent of Europe. Developed in Germany.
General Appearance: A dog of medium size, noble and steady, showing power, endurance and speed. Graceful outline and thoroughbred appearance.
Head: Clean cut, neither too light nor too heavy but well proportioned and clearly indicating whether it is a dog or a bitch. Skull sufficiently broad and slightly rounded. The furrow between the eyes not so deep and the occiput not so pronounced as in the English Pointer, nor is there such a definite stop. Lips fall almost vertically from somewhat protruding nose. Jaws powerful, scissors bite. Eyes of medium size, soft and intelligent, not protruding nor too deeply set, varying shades of brown to tone with coat. Ears broad and set high, neither too fleshy nor too thin. Nose brown.
Neck: Moderately long, muscular and slightly arched, becoming larger towards the shoulders. Skin should not fit loosely.
Body: Chest deep rather than wide, ribs deep and well sprung, but never barrel-shaped. Firm short back, not arched.
Legs and Feet: Shoulders sloping and very muscular. Upper arm bones between shoulder and elbow long. Elbows well laid back neither pointing outwards nor inwards. Hips broad. Thighs strong and well muscled. Feet compact, close-knit, round to spoon-shaped.
Tail: Docked by two-fifths to half its length.
Coat: Short, flat and coarse, slightly longer under the tail.
Colour: Solid liver, liver and white spotted, liver and white spotted and ticked, liver and white ticked, black and white.
Height and Weight: Dogs 62—64 cm, bitches rather less (minimum 58 cm); weight proportionate (25—30 kg).
Origin of Breed: By refinement of heavy, powerful, cumbersome dogs reliable in starting and tracking game.
Characteristics and Uses: Dual-purpose Pointer-Retriever which accounts for its excellence in the field, keen nose, perseverance in searching and enterprise. Equally good on land and in water. Should be owned by sportsmen only.

Polish Bracke (Ogar Polski)   85

Polish breed of gundog.
General Appearance: Moderately large, strongly built dog.
Head: Rather heavy, rectangular, fairly long with fine contours. Fleshy lips, jaws strong. Nose large, strong and dark. Eyes large, dark brown. Ears moderately long, set not too high, lying close to the head.
Neck: Moderately long, powerful nape, loose dewlap and a great many wrinkles.
Body: Chest deep, rib case long, well arched, rump long, broad and well muscled. Broad hind quarters which do not slope, capacious belly.
Legs and Feet: Strong, powerfully muscled, well proportioned, thighs long, hocks well let down, lean and well defined. Nails strong and short.
Tail: Thick, set not too high, slightly bent and slightly curled.
Coat: Coarse and rugged, longer on underside of tail.
Colour: Head and ears brownish, body black, dark grey or dark brown. White is also acceptable on head, chest, belly and tips of the feet and tail. An all black head is a serious fault.
Height and Weight: Dogs 56—65 cm, bitches 55—60 cm; dogs 25—32 kg, bitches 20—26 kg.
Origin of Breed: Original Polish breed.
Characteristics and Uses: Very persevering, passionate but rather heavy going gundog; intelligent, clean and teachable companion. When following a scent it should give tongue in a fairly high-pitched voice.

Weimaraner   100, 101

Systematically bred in Germany since the eighteenth century. Three varieties according to the type of coat: short-, long- or rough-haired.

General Appearance: Moderate to large sized sinewy gundog of working type, beautifully built.

Head: Moderately long with moderate stop. Rather prominent occipital bone and ears set well back. Foreface perfectly straight. Eyes amber or blue-grey, not protruding or too deeply set. Ears long and lobular. Nose flesh-coloured to grey.

Neck: Clean cut, moderately long, no dewlap.

Body: Chest well developed and deep. Back equal in length to height at withers. Topline of back level with slightly sloping croup. Abdomen firmly held, moderately tucked up flanks.

Legs and Feet: Forelegs straight and strong, hind legs moderately angulated. Feet firm and compact. No dewclaws.

Tail: Thickness of tail in proportion to the body. Set high, docked.

Coat: Short-haired should have short, smooth sleek coat. Long-haired should have a coat from 2.5 to 5 cm long. Rough-haired should have rough, harsh coat.

Colour: Preferably silver grey, shades of mouse or roe grey admissible.

Height and Weight: Dogs 59—70 cm, bitches 56—65 cm; weight not officially prescribed (23—28 kg).

Origin of Breed: Probably derived from an original old type of German pointer which came in mutations of silver grey.

Characteristics and Uses: Intelligent, easy to manage, not over temperamental. Excellent nose, quick to destroy vermin. Reliable pointer and willing to retrieve and work in water. Will persistently follow scent to the very end. Breeding presents no special difficulties. Is used as a service dog in some countries. Needs plenty of exercise.

German Long-haired Retriever   93

Gundog particularly adapted to work in woodland.

General Appearance: Dog with powerful muscular body, at the same time graceful to look at, with clean outlines and lively yet calm disposition.

Head: Long, dry and broad, divided equally between skull and muzzle, crown slightly domed.

Neck: Powerful, rising gracefully from chest and shoulders.

Body: Brisket deep, belly tucked in, back firm, straight and short, rising slightly at the shoulder, with strong loins.

Legs and Feet: Shoulder blades firmly placed, elbows extending in a backward direction, powerful rounded brisket. Shoulder blades and upper arm bones almost forming a right angle when in repose, upper arm bones and forearms forming a blunt angle. Hips, thighs and bones of the hock form a vertical line when viewed from behind.

Tail: Carried horizontally or slightly raised right at the tip, can be slightly docked.

Coat: On back and sides of brisket 3—5 cm long, on underside of neck, chest and belly somewhat longer, forming feathers on legs.

Colour: Brown or brown mixed with white.

Height and Weight: 58—68 cm; weight not officially prescribed (about 30 kg).

Origin of Breed: Developed from original old-German long-haired pointer.

Characteristics and Uses: Easy to manage, quick to learn, sharp, inborn talent for retrieving. Has all the qualities for all-round work. Very intelligent, faithful, devoted to its own family and affectionate, but suspicious of strangers. Coat requires a certain amount of care.

Small Münsterländer 68

Also known as the Moorland Spaniel — the smallest of the pointer and retriever breeds, particularly popular with town-dwelling sportsmen. A German breed.
General Appearance: Elegant, hardworking dog with strong physical constitution.
Head: Lean with only slightly defined stop. Eyes dark and deep set. Ears light weight, falling to a tip, very pliant. Nose with no white or flesh-coloured spots.
Neck: Slightly arched and strongly muscled.
Body: Straight, brisket deep, back strong and firm.
Legs and Feet: Straight and sturdy. Forelegs well angled, muscular thighs, firmly boned hocks. Compact feet.
Tail: Carried horizontally with the last third curving slightly upwards. Magnificent white or creamy feathering.
Coat: Smooth and flat, forming feathering on tail and legs and light fringes on the edges of the ears.
Colour: Brownish white, brown on the head usually with a blaze or star.
Height and Weight: Dogs 48—56 cm, bitches 44—52 cm; weight not officially prescribed (about 16 kg).
Origin of Breed: Result of the crossing of original old-German long-haired Pointer with some type of spaniel.
Characteristics and Uses: Highly intelligent, faithful, gentle and happy dog with an inborn talent for starting game and an excellent nose. Spaniel blood has tended to suppress its talent for setting and so it needs proper training in this from the very start. Otherwise it will set only for a short time and then start chasing game. Needs different handling and training from other gundogs.

Brittany Spaniel 64

One of a group of breeds of French long-haired gundogs.
General Appearance: Medium-sized, thickset but elegant, square-shaped, long-haired dog, with moderately long ears. Is either born tailless or has the tail docked.
Head: Muzzle shorter than the axis of the skull, straight or slightly snubbed. Nose as dark as possible. Rather square-shaped, fine lips, slightly upturned. Eyes dark amber, ears set high, on the short side, somewhat rounded with slight fringes and wavy hair.
Neck: Moderately long, lean, set well back from the shoulder blades.
Body: Back short, withers well developed, hind quarters short, broad and strong, rump sloping slightly downwards, brisket deep and capacious reaching nearly to the elbows.
Legs and Feet: Forelegs very straight, fine, muscular and slightly feathered. Thighs broad, angle of hocks not too open, feathering to half way down the thighs. Feet compact.
Tail: Carried level with the back or slightly downwards, slight wave at the tip, docked to 10 cm if not born with a short tail.
Coat: Fairly fine, predominantly smooth or slightly wavy.
Colour: White and orange, white and chestnut, white and black, tricolour or flecked with some of these colours.
Height and Weight: Ideal height for dogs 48—50 cm, for bitches 47—49 cm; weight not officially prescribed (13—15 kg).
Origin of Breed: Descended from original breed.
Characteristics and Uses: Pleasing, very lively dog with energetic movements and intelligent expression. Well-tried gundog.

Pudelpointer   88

Unusually fine German breed of rough-coated gundog.
General Appearance: Heavy type of dog with wiry coat.
Head: Moderately long, wide, coated with wiry hair, with beard and large eyebrows. Very clearly defined stop. Muzzle rather similar to the concave one of the Pointer. Eyes with the expression of a bird of prey. Fairly large ears lying flat against the face.
Neck: Medium length, lean, muscular, arched.
Body: Back short and level, shoulders and hind quarters broad. Withers high, long and full. Brisket rather broad and very deep. Belly tucked up towards the back.
Legs and Feet: Forelegs straight, shoulders sloping, broad, long and lying flat. Muscles on shoulders clearly visible. Bones of hind legs well angulated, muscles firm and long. Feet round.
Tail: Light, carried level with the back, no feathering, docked.
Coat: Medium length, harsh, dense and wiry.
Colour: Brown or russet.
Height and Weight: Dogs 58—65 cm, bitches 56—63 cm; weight not officially prescribed.
Origin of Breed: Result of the crossing of the English Pointer with the Poodle.
Characteristics and Uses: Intelligent, teachable, faithful, with outstanding talent as an all-round gundog, excells at pointing game. There can be a wide variety in one litter, some pups having the long coat of the poodle, others the short coat of the pointer.

German Wire-haired Pointer   91

One of the most popular German breeds of gundog on the continent of Europe, gaining popularity in America.
General Appearance: Moderately large, elegant, not very conspicuously coloured gundog, full of keenness.
Head: Fairly long with broad, long muzzle, strong teeth, moderately long ears and clear eyes.
Neck: Moderately long and thick.
Body: Withers high and long. Brisket deep, ribs well sprung. Back short and straight, loins muscular, hips broad. Rump long, slightly slanting, well muscled, belly tucked up. Ratio of length of body to height at the shoulder 10 : 9.
Legs and Feet: Viewed from front and rear vertical, well angled. Shoulder blades lying flat. Feet round.
Tail: Docked.
Coat: Very harsh, moderately long, wiry and flat. Beard not particularly long.
Colour: Inconspicuously brown.
Height and Weight: Dogs 60—67 cm, bitches 56—62 cm; weight not officially prescribed.
Origin of Breed: Descended from various pointer breeds, especially rough-haired.
Characteristics and Uses: All-round gundog as well as faithful, affectionate and devoted family companion but wary of strangers. Should only be kept as a gundog. Coat requires no special care.

Czech Whiskers (Wire-haired Pointer) 92

All-round working gundog, very hardy, quick to destroy vermin. Developed in Czechoslovakia.

General Appearance: Medium-sized, rough-haired dog.

Head: Lean, rather narrow and long, head carried high on the neck. Muzzle slightly convex, dark brown, upper lip slightly overhanging. Eyes almond-shaped, dark amber to deep chestnut. Ears set high with broad base.

Neck: Moderately long, set high at the withers, nape slightly arched.

Body: Back short, firm, sloping down to the rump from well defined withers. Loins short, rather wide and slightly arched. Belly somewhat tucked up, rump slightly sloping.

Legs and Feet: Shoulders well muscled, forearm upright and straight. Pelvis proportionately long, thighs broad. Feet spoon-shaped.

Tail: Fairly thick, docked by three-fifths of its length.

Coat: Outercoat 3—4 cm long, comparatively hard and rough.

Colour: Off-white with or without brown patches, brown with flecks on the chest and lower part of forelegs or brown with no markings.

Height and Weight: Dogs 60—66 cm, bitches 58—62 cm; dogs 28—34 kg, bitches 22—28 kg.

Origin of Breed: Crossing of original wire-haired pointer with other pointer breeds.

Characteristics and Uses: Hardy, easy to manage, faithful and affectionate to its own family, rather fierce with strangers. Good all-round gundog. Coat needs no special care.

German Rough-haired Pointer (Retriever) 96

One of the oldest of rough-haired gundogs bred in Germany.

General Appearance: Moderately large, powerful but by no means cumbersome dog with dropped ears and docked tail.

Head: Medium-sized, muzzle moderately long, well closed lips, bridge of nose long, broad and straight, gently rising stop, occipital crest not over developed. Nose according to colour of coat — either dark or light brown. Eyes also brown or lighter. Ears moderately long.

Neck: Strong, moderately long, slightly arched.

Body: Back level, broad and muscular, broad short loins, brisket deep, ribs well sprung, belly tucked in.

Legs and Feet: Forelegs straight, well muscled, shoulders slanting, elbows neither turned in nor out. Hind legs muscular, set not too straight, not too slanting. Feet round.

Tail: Moderately long, carried horizontally or slightly raised, may be docked but not too much.

Coat: Harsh, straight and coarse. Thick beard and eyebrows, slight fringes on the back of the legs.

Colour: Brown and white, greyish brown with rather large brown patches.

Height and Weight: Dogs 60—66 cm, bitches slightly less; weight not officially prescribed.

Origin of Breed: Descended from original breed.

Characteristics and Uses: Intelligent, serious and sensible, all-round gundog. Also a good watchdog and pleasant companion. Should only be kept by sportsmen.

Fox Terrier   41, 43

A dog which in the past would follow a fox to earth, without fear of the dark unfamiliar surroundings, entering, without hesitation, into combat with an equally heavy and well armed enemy which is fighting for its life. An English breed.

General Appearance: Small, lively dog with a well proportioned body on proportionately long legs, and a hard coat in which white predominates.

Head: Skull should be flat and moderately narrow, slightly sloping. Muzzle gradually decreasing in width from eyes to nose, but should not go down in a straight line like a wedge. Not much stop. Jaw strong and muscular with strong white teeth, the lower canines dovetailing with the upper, the tips of the upper incisors slightly extending over the lower. Nose black. Eyes dark and rather deep set. Ears small, V-shaped, moderately thick, dropping forward close to the cheeks.

Neck: Should be clean and muscular, fairly long without throatiness, gradually widening to the shoulders, forming a graceful line.

Body: Back short and level, loins strong and muscular, slightly arched. Chest deep, fore-ribs moderately arched, back ribs deep. The shorter the Fox Terrier's body the better; a bitch can be a little longer than a dog.

Legs and Feet: Shoulders long and sloping, well laid back from clean cut withers. Elbows are held flat to the body and in movement travel straight forward. Hind legs strong and muscular, quite free of droop or crouch. Feet round, compact and not too large.

Tail: Of good strength with thick coat, carried gaily but not over the back or curled, docked to about three-quarters.

Coat: In smooth-haired variety (below) flat, smooth and hard, in wire-haired variety (above) a tendency to twist.

Colour: White should predominate. Brindle, red, blue or liver markings are a fault.

Height and Weight: Dogs 38—40 cm, bitches 36—38 cm; weight not officially prescribed.

Origin of Breed: Descended from terriers kept by the masters of fox-hunting, who used them for bolting foxes that had gone to earth to escape the hounds. The white colour came to be preferred as it more easily distinguished the terrier from its quarry the fox. The docked tail was supposed to make a convenient handle by which the dog could be pulled from the earth.

Characteristics and Uses: The Fox Terrier is a very excitable, alert and playful dog. It tends to be both noisy and aggressive with other dogs and is therefore not a dog for people with weak nerves. Like many terriers it is very active, courageous and difficult to control. The wire-haired variety needs considerable trimming if it is to look smart.

Bull Terrier 63

Moderate-sized, short-haired, tenacious sporting terrier of English origin, comparatively insensitive to wounds.
General Appearance: Strong, well proportioned, muscular and very active dog.
Head: Oval, almost egg-shaped, comparatively long and very deep. The profile of the head from the crest of the occiput to the nose is almost arc-shaped. Eyes as dark as possible, obliquely placed and close set. Ears stiffly erect, small and thin.
Neck: Moderately long, arched, very muscular.
Body: Back short, strong and muscular, chest broad from the front, brisket of great depth. Ribs well sprung, roaching towards the loins.
Legs and Feet: Moderately long and perfectly parallel, making it possible to stand solidly. Round, compact, cat-like feet.
Tail: Comparatively short, thick at the root, should taper to a fine point, set low and carried horizontally.
Coat: Short, flat, even harsh with a fine gloss.
Colour: White, brindle. All white individuals should have pure white coat from the ears back. In coloured specimens, the colour, preferably brindle, should predominate over white.
Height and Weight: 40—55 cm; dogs 20—30 kg, bitches 15—26 kg.
Origin of Breed: Result of crossing Bulldog with Terrier.
Characteristics and Uses: Faithful and affectionate especially to children, excellent guard dog. Requires from puppyhood gentle but firm and consistent treatment, as it can be aggressive to other dogs.

Welsh Terrier 39

One of the oldest terrier breeds originating in Great Britain.
General Appearance: Medium-sized dog full of fire, looks like a small edition of the Airedale Terrier.
Head: Long and symmetrical, skull rather flat, narrow between the ears; should not be sunken beneath or between the eyes. Eyes small, well set in, dark. Ears V-shaped, small, carried forward close to the cheek.
Neck: Of moderate length and thickness, slightly arched.
Body: Short back, well ribbed up, loins strong and deep, moderately wide chest.
Legs and Feet: Forelegs straight and muscular with well developed bones, hind legs strong with muscular rather long thighs. Feet small, round and cat-like.
Tail: Well set on, but not too gaily carried, docked.
Coat: Wiry, hard, very close and abundant.
Colour: Black and tan or black grizzle and tan is preferred.
Height and Weight: Dogs up to 40 cm, bitches rather less; 9—9.5 kg.
Origin of Breed: Descended from original Welsh dog used as watchdog and for hunting.
Characteristics and Uses: Eager hunter, agreeable and affectionate, obedient and anxious to please, always gay and easily managed. Ideal pet for town-dwellers. Needs plenty of exercise and to be kept busy. Coat needs trimming.

Boston Terrier 57

An American breed resembling the small, lightweight bulldog.
General Appearance: Medium-sized dog with short, fine coat and a short tail.
Head: Skull flat, square; cheeks flat, abrupt brow, clearly defined stop. No wrinkles. Eyes large, round, dark in colour. Ears set erect, small and thin. Nose not too wide, well defined line between the nostrils.
Neck: Moderately long, slightly arched, gracefully carrying the head.
Body: Deep chest, short back, deep, well sprung ribs. Loins short, muscled, rump slightly curved.
Legs and Feet: Forelegs straight and well muscled, short pasterns, sloping shoulders. Elbows turned neither in nor out. Feet round, compact.
Tail: Set low, short, with no feathers or rough hair, carried horizontally.
Coat: Short, glossy, of fine texture.
Colour: Evenly distributed brindle with white markings. Black with white markings also permissible. Black, black and tan, liver or grey colour are faults.
Height and Weight: Height not officially prescribed, weight should not exceed 11 kg in any case. The breed is divided by classes into lightweight (under 6.8 kg), middleweight (6.8—9 kg) and heavyweight (9—11 kg).
Origin of Breed: Developed in the late nineteenth century by crossing the bulldog and the white English terrier.
Characteristics and Uses: Lively, intelligent, amiable dog, popular especially in the USA as a faithful family companion.

Irish Terrier 52

Typical terrier both as regards exterior appearance and temperament. Developed in Ireland.
General Appearance: Strong, lithe medium-sized dog with graceful 'racing outline', rather small ears and docked tail.
Head: Long, skull flat and rather narrow between ears, getting slightly narrower towards the eye, free from wrinkles, stop hardly visible. Jaw strong and muscular, scissors bite. Eyes dark and small. Ears small, V-shaped, drooping forward closely to the cheek.
Neck: Of fair length, widening towards the shoulders, free of throatiness, well carried.
Body: Moderately long, chest deep and muscular, back strong and straight.
Legs and Feet: Forelegs moderately long, well set from the shoulders, straight with plenty of bone and muscle. Hind legs strong and muscular, moving straight forward. Feet strong and rounded.
Tail: Docked to about three-quarters, free of fringe or feather.
Coat: Hard and wiry, having a broken appearance.
Colour: Bright red, red wheaten or yellow-red.
Height and Weight: About 45 cm; dogs 12 kg, bitches 11 kg.
Origin of Breed: The Irish Terrier gained its present appearance about 100 years ago as a result of the determined efforts of breeders.
Characteristics and Uses: Full of fire, affectionate and devoted but can be obstinate. Used to kill vermin and to start and retrieve game but at the same time an excellent companion. Needs plenty of exercise and an owner with calm nerves.

Kerry Blue Terrier 59

This breed was first shown in England in 1922.

General Appearance: Medium-sized, upstanding, well knit and well proportioned dog.

Head:.Long with only a slight stop, flat over the skull. Jaw very strong, deep and punishing. Eyes dark, small to medium-sized. Ears medium-sized, V-shaped, carried forward.

Neck: Strong and reachy, forming a smooth line with sloping shoulders.

Body: Short, coupled with brisket of good depth and well sprung ribs. Topline level.

Legs and Feet: Legs straight, bones powerful. Front straight, neither too wide nor too narrow. Feet round and small.

Tail: Set high, carried erect, docked.

Coat: Soft, silky, plentiful and wavy.

Colour: Any shade of blue with or without black points. Small white patch on chest should not be penalized.

Height and Weight: Dogs 45.5—48 cm, bitches slightly less; dogs 14.5—16.5 kg, bitches proportionately less.

Origin of Breed: The origin of the Kerry Blue is not completely clear. All that is certain is that it comes from Ireland.

Characteristics and Uses: Faithful, alert, affectionate and easily trained, today more of a pet than a sporting terrier. Needs a firm hand because, like most terriers, it is intolerant of other dogs.

Airedale Terrier 81

The biggest of the terriers and an all-round working dog, bred in Britain.

General Appearance: Moderately large, elegant dog.

Head: Skull long and flat, not too broad between the ears. Powerful jaws, flat lips, foreface well filled in. Black nose. Eyes dark and small. Ears V-shaped, comparatively small with wide carriage.

Neck: Clean, muscular, moderate length, free from throatiness.

Body: Back short, strong and level, muscular hind quarters, ribs well sprung, chest deep but not broad.

Legs and Feet: Forelegs perfectly straight with plenty of bone. Hind legs long and muscular, with strong thighs and muscular second thighs. Feet small, round and compact.

Tail: Set high, carried gaily, docked to fair length.

Coat: Hard, dense and wiry, not too long, should lie straight and close to the body.

Colour: Body black or dark grey, head, ears and legs as far as thighs and elbows tan.

Height and Weight: Dogs 58.5—61 cm, bitches 56—58.5 cm; weight commensurate with height and type (20—22 kg).

Origin of Breed: Crossing of various terrier breeds and possibly Gordon Setter and Retriever.

Characteristics and Uses: All-round hunting, service, guide dog and pet. Good-natured, reliable and full of keenness. Needs plenty of exercise and to be kept busy.

Bedlington Terrier 46

One of the oldest of the terrier breeds.
General Appearance: Medium-sized, graceful, slender, well muscled dog.
Head: Narrow but deep and rounded. Jaws strong and tapering. There should be no stop and the line from the occiput to the end of the nose should be straight and unbroken. Eyes small, bright and well sunk. Ears moderate-sized, nut-shaped, set low and lying flat to the cheek. Blues and blue-and-tans have black noses, livers and sandies have brown.
Neck: Long, deep at the base and tapering towards the head.
Body: Muscular, deep through the brisket. The back should be roached and markedly arched.
Legs and Feet: Forelegs should be straight, wider apart at the chest than at the feet. Hind legs well muscled and moderately long. Long hare-like feet.
Tail: Of moderate length, thick at the root, tapering to a point, gracefully curved, never held over the back.
Coat: Thick and linty, not wiry.
Colour: Blue, blue and tan, liver, sandy.
Height and Weight: Dogs about 41 cm, bitches rather less tall; 8—10 kg.
Origin of Breed: Developed from original dog bred near the borders of England and Scotland.
Characteristics and Uses: Keen, nimble, bold but docile, an instinctive hunter of vermin, watchful but at the same time an amiable and faithful companion. Popular as a pet but can be used for hunting and guard duties. Needs a great deal of exercise and careful trimming.

German Hunt Terrier 42

A dark coloured dog used for hunting vermin and going to earth. Bred in Germany.
General Appearance: Long in back with rather long legs, dropped ears and docked tail.
Head: Skull flat without sharply defined stop, powerful muzzle. Nose black or brown. Eyes dark and small. Ears V-shaped, set high, lying lightly on the cheeks.
Neck: Strong, with marked transition to shoulders.
Body: Back strong and straight but not too short, brisket deep and arched, loins and rump muscular.
Legs and Feet: Shoulder blades long, slanting, pasterns slightly angled, bones on the strong side. Hind legs with long, well angled and muscular thighs and low set hocks. Forefeet broader than hind.
Tail: Well set on, carried somewhat slantwise to the back.
Coat: Straight, dense, hard and harsh or thick and rough.
Colour: Main colour black, grizzle or dark brown with tan markings.
Height and Weight: Up to 40 cm; dogs 9—10 kg, bitches 7—8 kg.
Origin of Breed: By crossing of the Fox Terrier, Lakeland Terrier and other dark-coloured terriers.
Characteristics and Uses: Intelligent, lively, sharp, wary, pleasant family companion, passionate hunter, sharp and noisy when following a scent. Needs plenty of exercise.

Scottish Terrier   15

Today kept as a pet rather than for hunting vermin.
General Appearance: Low, rough-haired, comparatively long head and high set ears.
Head: Long, skull nearly flat, slight but distinct stop between skull and foreface. Nose large. Eyes almond-shaped, dark brown. Ears neat, of fine texture, pointed and erect.
Neck: Muscular and of moderate length.
Body: Brisket comparatively broad and rather deep, ribs well rounded, back comparatively short and well muscled, broad muscular loins.
Legs and Feet: Forelegs straight and well boned to straight pasterns, hind legs exceptionally strong, thighs long and muscular, hocks strong and well bent. Feet of good size, toes well arched, close knit.
Tail: Of moderate length, carried straight or slightly bent.
Coat: Short, dense with short soft undercoat and harsh, hard, wiry outercoat.
Colour: Black, wheaten or brindle.
Height and Weight: 25.5—28 cm; 8.5—10.5 kg.
Origin of Breed: Original British terrier breed, improved to its present striking form.
Characteristics and Uses: Full of temperament, clever, wary, faithful, lively dog, loving human companionship. Excellent for going to earth and scenting. Not particularly exacting to breed, though sometimes there are whelping difficulties due to angle of the pelvis.

Sealyham Terrier   23

A terrier for destroying vermin created in the mid-19th century by Captain John Edwards and named after his estate in South Wales.
General Appearance: Short-legged, rough-haired terrier with a docked tail.
Head: Skull slightly domed, wide between the ears. Jaws powerful and long, scissors bite. Nose black. Eyes dark, round and medium-sized. Ears medium-sized, carried at side of cheek.
Neck: Fairly long, thick and muscular.
Body: Medium length, flexible, level, ribs well sprung, chest broad and deep and well let down between the forelegs.
Legs and Feet: Forelegs strong, short and straight. Hind legs very strong, thighs deep, muscular, strong hocks. Feet round and cat-like with thick pads.
Tail: Docked and carried erect.
Coat: Long, harsh and wiry.
Colour: White, white and lemon, brown markings or badger pied markings on head and ears.
Height and Weight: Should not exceed 30 cm; dogs up to 9 kg, bitches up to 8 kg.
Origin of Breed: Created by Captain Edwards from the most courageous, hardworking terriers he could find.
Characteristics and Uses: Intelligent, quiet, at the same time sharp and watchful, tough, hardworking dog which can compare with any other terrier. Well suited for urban life because it is a very agreeable, affectionate dog and does not require a great deal of exercise. Coat needs trimming.

Czech Terrier   24

A sporting terrier developed in Czechoslovakia after the Second World War.
General Appearance: Short-legged dog with a not very striking exterior but excellent hunting abilities.
Head: Comparatively long, bridge of nose straight, stop scarcely perceptible, forming a blunt but not broad wedge. Eyes medium-sized. Ears also medium-sized, pendent, almost covering the ear orifice.
Neck: Moderately long, carried diagonally, strong and without dewlap.
Body: Line of the back level, brisket barrel-shaped rather than deep, belly only slightly tucked in.
Legs and Feet: Forelegs move directly ahead from the axis of the body. Hind legs parallel with strong movement.
Tail: 18—20 cm long, rather thick, in repose carried directly downwards.
Coat: Dense with silky gloss, trimmed by clipping.
Colour: Blue-grey or café au lait. In both colours yellow, grey and white markings are allowed.
Height and Weight: 27—34 cm; 6—9 kg.
Origin of Breed: By crossing of Scottish Terrier and Sealyham Terrier amongst others.
Characteristics and Uses: Very active, keen and easily managed, enthusiastic, good-natured and affectionate, but keen vermin killer. Good for going to earth and surface work. Needs no special care.

Skye Terrier   9

Most striking of the terrier family both as regards body structure and coat.
General Appearance: Long, short-legged dog with long, dense, silky coat.
Head: Long, with powerful jaw. Eyes brown, medium-sized, close set. Ears prick or drop.
Neck: Long and slightly arched.
Body: Long and low, back level, ribs well sprung giving a flattish appearance.
Legs and Feet: Short and muscular. Feet large and pointing forward.
Tail: When hanging upper part pendulous and lower half thrown back in a curve. When raised, continues the line of the back.
Coat: Double. Undercoat short, close, soft and woolly, outercoat long, hard and flat, free of curl.
Colour: Dark or light blue-grey, fawn, creamy yellow with black points.
Height and Weight: Dogs up to 25 cm, bitches smaller; 11.3 kg.
Origin of Breed: The Skye Terrier comes from the Island of Skye in the Hebrides. Appears to have been crossed with other breeds to produce the present type.
Characteristics and Uses: Has maintained excellent hunting instincts but is now seldom used for this purpose. Particularly popular as a pet, fond of its own family, including children, but does not tolerate strangers and is very reserved with them. Coat needs a great deal of care if the dog is not to lose its principal decorative asset.

West Highland White Terrier 19

Comes from Scotland and the Hebrides.
General Appearance: Small, game, with no small amount of self-esteem, fearless terrier with a very lively expression.
Head: Slightly domed, thickly coated with hair, carried at a right angle or less to the axis of the neck. Distinct stop. Eyes widely set. Ears small, erect, terminating in a sharp point.
Neck: Muscular, gradually thickening towards the base.
Body: Back straight, loins broad and strong, chest deep, ribs well arched in upper half.
Legs and Feet: Forelegs short, muscular, straight and sinewy, thickly covered with short hard hair, hind legs short, muscular and sinewy. Forefeet longer than hind ones.
Tail: 12.5—15 cm long, carried jauntily but not over the back, not docked.
Coat: Outercoat hard, about 5 cm long, undercoat soft and flat.
Colour: Pure white.
Height and Weight: About 28 cm; weight not officially prescribed.
Origin of Breed: Believed to be descended from white puppies in litters of Cairn or Scottish Terriers.
Characteristics and Uses: Affectionate pet but also used for digging out foxes and for otter hunting. Has won the heart of many breeders for its sweet nature, cleverness and happy disposition.

Cairn Terrier 10

One of the smallest of terrier breeds.
General Appearance: Small, low built dog, always gay and bearing a shaggy coat.
Head: Small, foxy, skull broad in proportion, strong jaws, well defined stop, strong muzzle. Decided indentation between the eyes, hair should be full on forehead. Eyes moderate-sized, dark hazel, shaggy eyebrows. Ears small, pointed and carried erect.
Neck: Well set on but not too short.
Body: Compact, back straight, medium in length, well sprung deep ribs, strong sinews.
Legs and Feet: Forelegs of medium length, covered with hard hair, sloping shoulders, should not turn out at elbow, hind legs very muscular. Forefeet larger than hind, can be slightly turned out.
Tail: Short, well furnished with hair but not too feathery, carried gaily but should not turn over the back.
Coat: Undercoat short and close, outercoat profuse, hard but not coarse.
Colour: Red, sandy, grey, brindle or nearly black. Dark points on ears and muzzle.
Height and Weight: 23—25 cm; about 6.5 kg.
Origin of Breed: Perfected from original British breed.
Characteristics and Uses: Lively, courageous, always cheerful, clever, affectionate, nice to look at, courageous at digging out vermin and at the same time an agreeable family dog.

Yorkshire Terrier 8

Among the smallest of the terriers. Developed in England.

General Appearance: Toy terrier with long, flowing coat parted down the length of the body from the nose to the tip of the tail.

Head: Small, flat, not too prominent or round in the skull. Perfectly black nose. Eyes medium-sized, dark and sparkling. Small V-shaped ears either carried erect or semi-erect, covered with short, thick hair of deep brown colour.

Neck: Slender and well set.

Body: Very compact with a good loin, topline of the back straight.

Legs and Feet: Quite straight, well covered with hair of rich golden tan. Feet as round as possible.

Tail: Docked by half its length with plenty of hair.

Coat: Moderately long, straight and glossy, of a fine silky texture.

Colour: From the occiput to the root of the tail dark steel blue (must never be mixed with fawn, bronze or dark hairs). All tan hairs should be darker at the roots than in the middle, shading to a still lighter tone at the tips.

Height and Weight: Height not officially prescribed; up to 3 kg.

Origin of Breed: Believed to have originated from the crossing of several breeds. Most often the Skye Terrier or Maltese are cited as its ancestors.

Characteristics and Uses: Lively, merry, affectionate, intelligent and self-confident little dog. Bred just as a pet. Coat needs special care.

Tibetan Terrier 38

A dog not unlike an Old English Sheepdog in miniature. Comes from Tibet.

General Appearance: Well muscled, medium-sized dog with long coat.

Head: Skull of medium length, narrowing slightly from ear to eye. The cheek bones are curved but should not bulge. Marked stop in front of eyes. Muzzle not too massive. Scissors bite but should not be penalized if slightly undershot. Nose black. Eyes large and dark. Ears pendent, not too close to head, V-shaped.

Neck: Moderately long, thickly coated with hair.

Body: Compact. Length from point of shoulder to root of tail equal to height at the shoulder. Well ribbed up. Loin slightly arched.

Legs and Feet: Forelegs parallel, heavily furnished. Hind legs should be slightly longer than forelegs with well bent stifles and low set hocks. Feet large, round, heavily furnished with hair between the toes and pads.

Tail: Medium length, set fairly high and carried in a gay curl over the back. Well feathered. There is often a kink near the tip.

Coat: Double coated. Top coat profuse, either straight or waved, long hair falling forward over the eyes. Lower jaw should carry a small amount of beard.

Colour: White, golden, cream, grey or smoke, black, particolour and tricolour.

Height and Weight: Dogs 35.5—40.5 cm, bitches slightly smaller; weight not officially prescribed.

Origin of Breed: Original breed from the mountainous regions of central Asia.

Characteristics and Uses: Alert, intelligent and game. Not fierce or pugnacious. In its native land used as a herding dog, elsewhere becoming popular as a house dog.

Dachshund 3, 4, 5, 6, 7

German sporting dog once used for tracking badgers and foxes when they have gone to earth and for bolting them. It comes in three varieties: Smooth-haired, long-haired and wire-haired and in two sizes: Standard and Miniature. On the continent of Europe Toy Dachshunds are also recognized.

General Appearance: Long and low with compact well muscled body, head carried erect, intelligent expression.

Head: Long and appearing conical when seen from above, from a side view tapering to the point of the muzzle. Stop not pronounced, skull slightly arched in profile. Scissors or level bite. Eyes medium in size, oval and set obliquely. Ears broad, of moderate length and well rounded, high and well set on.

Neck: Sufficiently long, muscular, clean, no dewlap, slightly arched in the nape, carried well up and forward.

Body: Long and muscular, slightly depressed at shoulders and slightly arched over the loin. Breast bone strong and prominent. Looked at from the front the thorax should be oval allowing ample room for heart and lungs. Moderately tucked up belly.

Legs and Feet: Shoulder blades long, broad and firmly placed on a robust rib cage. Upper arm the same length as shoulder blades. Forearm comparatively short. Pelvis strong, set obliquely. Upper thigh set at right angles to the pelvis is strong and of good length. Toes compact and well arched. Hind feet smaller than forefeet.

Tail: Set fairly high, strong and tapering, not too long, not too curved or carried too high.

Coat and Colour:

Smooth-haired Dachshund:

Coat: Short, dense, smooth but strong.

Colour: Any colour other than white (except a white spot on the breast). Nose and nails should be black. In red dogs a red nose is permissible, but not desirable. In chocolates and dapples the nose may be brown or flesh-coloured. In dapples the dog should be evenly dappled all over.

Long-haired Dachshund:

Coat: Soft and straight or slightly waved, of shining colour, longer under the neck, the underparts of the body and on the ears, behind the legs where it should develop into abundant feathering, and on the tail where it should form a flag.

Colour: Black and tan, dark brown with lighter shadings, dark red, light red, dappled, tiger-marked or brindle.

Wire-haired Dachshund:

Coat: With the exception of the jaw, eyebrows and ears, the whole body is covered with a completely even, short, harsh coat and an undercoat. There should be a beard on the chin. The eyebrows are bushy and the hair on the ears almost smooth.

Colour: All colours are allowed but a white patch on the chest though not a fault is not desirable.

Height and Weight: Heavy type: dogs over 7 kg, bitches over 6.5 kg. Light type: dogs up to 7 kg, bitches up to 6 kg. Miniature: dogs up to 4 kg, bitches up to 3.5 kg. Miniature: chest circumference 35 cm. Toy: chest circumference 30 cm. Height commensurate to weight.

Origin of Breed: Derived from the German Bracke.

Characteristics and Uses: Clever sporting dog, lively, courageous and obedient if well trained. It is inclined to be independent and therefore training should start earlier than with other sporting breeds. Especially suitable for going to ground because of its low build, very strong forequarters and forelegs and the immense power of its bite and hold. Remarkably adaptable and makes an agreeable and affectionate pet.

Golden Retriever 80

One of the commonest of all the retrievers.
General Appearance: Medium-sized, powerful but not clumsy, solidly built dog with a kind expression.
Head: Skull broad, well set on a straight neck. Muzzle wide, strong jaws, good stop. Eyes dark, of a very kind expression; eyelids dark-rimmed. Ears medium-sized, well set on. Nose black. Neither overshot nor undershot.
Neck: Straight and muscular.
Body: Well balanced, short; chest broad, ribs deep and well sprung.
Legs and Feet: Forelegs straight, well boned, long shoulders. Loins and hind legs strong and muscular. Not cow-hocked. Feet round.
Tail: Carried not too gaily, tip not curled.
Coat: Smooth or wavy, abundant feathering and dense waterproof undercoat.
Colour: All golden and cream shades are permissible, but no red or mahogany. White hairs on the chest also permissible.
Height and Weight: Dogs 56—61 cm, bitches 51—56 cm; average weight of dogs should be 29.5—31.5 kg, of bitches 25—27 kg.
Origin of Breed: An original English breed, probably with an admixture of other breeds' blood.
Characteristics and Uses: Active, intelligent and amiable dog, specialized in retrieving.

Labrador Retriever 74

The oldest and most popular of breeds of gundog specializing in retrieving game. An English breed.
General Appearance: Medium-sized, short-haired dog with drop ears and moderately long thick tail.
Head: Clean cut, skull broad with a pronounced stop, jaws of medium length, powerful, lips not fleshy, scissors bite. Nose broad. Eyes medium-sized, brown or hazel. Ears flat to the head, carried rather backwards.
Neck: Clean, strong and powerful, set into well placed shoulders.
Body: Back short and coupled, brisket appropriately deep and broad with well sprung ribs, robust loins.
Legs and Feet: Straight, well muscled, shoulders long and sloping, hocks well angled. Feet close and compact.
Tail: Very thick towards the base, tapering towards the tip, covered with short hard hair, carried gaily but should not be curled over the back.
Coat: Short, thick, not curly, harsh to the touch.
Colour: Generally black, liver, yellow of various shades, fox red, cream without white markings.
Height and Weight: Dogs 55—57 cm, bitches 54—56 cm; weight not officially prescribed.
Origin of Breed: Descended from original breed from Newfoundland.
Characteristics and Uses: Intelligent, alert, amenable, very lively but at the same time a deliberate dog, a fine example of a retriever and also a very good family companion. Used as a guide dog for the blind and a service dog.

Greyhound 110

The fastest of all racing dogs. Can develop a speed of up to 50 km per hour over short distances. Developed in the Middle East.

General Appearance: Strongly built, upstanding dog of generous proportions, muscular power and symmetrical formation.

Head: Long, of moderate width, with flat skull, slight stop. Eyes bright and intelligent, dark in colour. Ears small, rose-shaped.

Neck: Long, muscular, elegantly arched.

Body: Chest deep and capacious, ribs deep, well sprung and carried well back. Back long, broad and square. Loin powerful, slightly arched. Shoulders clearly defined.

Legs and Feet: Forelegs long and straight, bone of good substance and quality. Thighs and second thighs wide and muscular, showing great propelling power. Feet of moderate length, compact.

Tail: Long, set low, carried low, slightly curved.

Coat: Fine and close.

Colour: Black, white, red, blue, fawn, fallow, brindle or any of the colours broken with white.

Height and Weight: 66—69 cm, sometimes over; weight in proportion (about 25 kg).

Origin of Breed: The ancestors of the Greyhound of today came from North Africa.

Characteristics and Uses: Intelligence comparable with that of other breeds, gentle but can be fierce. Racing dog with rather a complicated disposition. Needs a good deal of exercise and is not easy to manage. Training requires a sensitive approach.

Whippet 55

Miniature version of the Greyhound but with more fire.

General Appearance: Very elegant dog with graceful, symmetrical proportions, well muscled and proudly held body.

Head: Long and lean, flat on top, tapering to the muzzle, rather wide between the eyes. Jaws powerful and clean cut. Eyes bright and alert. Ears rose-shaped, small and fine in texture.

Neck: Long and muscular, elegantly arched.

Body: Back broad, firm, muscular, somewhat long. Slightly arched over the loin. Brisket very deep, muscles well formed. Loin gives the impression of strength and power.

Legs and Feet: Forelegs straight and upright, front not too wide, elbows well set under the body, pasterns strong with slight spring. Broad across the thighs, stifles well bent, hocks well let down, second thighs strong. Feet very neat, knuckles highly arched.

Tail: No feathering, when in action carried up in a delicate curve.

Coat: Fine, short and close.

Colour: Any colour or mixture of colours.

Height and Weight: Dogs 42—50 cm (ideal height 47 cm), bitches up to 44.5 cm; dogs 10 kg, bitches about 9 kg.

Origin of Breed: This smaller edition of the Greyhound was developed for rabbit coursing and for racing by the colliers in the north of England during the first half of the nineteenth century.

Characteristics and Uses: Keen, speedy, eager, intelligent and good-natured, affectionate, fond of children. Typical racing dog but also makes a good pet. Needs a great deal of exercise.

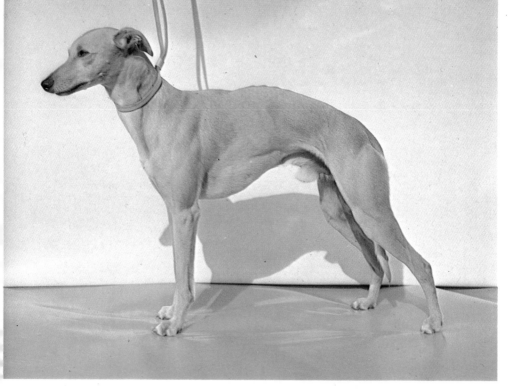

Sloughi   104

One of the oldest breeds of Moroccan origin, runs like a gazelle and can develop a speed of up to 60 km per hour.

General Appearance: Tall, elegant, short-haired sight hound, very similar to the Greyhound.

Head: More akin to that of the jackal than the Greyhound, skull flat and rather broad between the ears, stop only slightly defined, muzzle tapering to a point, the length corresponding to the length of the skull. Nose black. Eyes large and dark. Ears moderately large, lying close to the head, pendent.

Neck: Moderately long and lean.

Body: Back comparatively short, withers not well defined, rump falling slantwise, hip bones clearly projecting, brisket deep, belly tucked in.

Legs and Feet: Straight, exceptionally long, shoulder blades slightly slanting, dry, flat, thighs very muscular, long, broad and rather flat. Feet comparatively long.

Tail: Long, thin, hooked or curled.

Coat: Dense, short, fine.

Colour: Usually light sandy with dark rust mask and eyebrows.

Height and Weight: 60—70 cm; weight not officially prescribed.

Origin of Breed: Descended from original Arab breed.

Characteristics and Uses: Carries itself with great self-confidence. Devoted only to its own master but even with him is not very demonstrative. Extremely suspicious of strangers. In its North African and Arab homelands is used for hunting hare, gazelle and antelope. Needs a great deal of exercise.

Italian Greyhound   33

The smallest breed of sight hound, a miniature replica of the Greyhound.

General Appearance: Small, long-legged, slender, elegant dog with short coat and characteristic high stepping free action.

Head: Skull long, flat and narrow, muzzle very fine. Nose dark. Eyes rather large, bright and full of expression. Ears rose-shaped, placed well back. Teeth level.

Neck: Long and gracefully arched.

Body: Back curved and drooping at the hind quarters. Chest deep and narrow. Belly tucked in.

Legs and Feet: Shoulders long and sloping, forelegs straight. Thighs muscular. Hocks well let down. Long hare feet.

Tail: Rather long and fine with low carriage.

Coat: Skin fine and supple. Hair thin and glossy.

Colour: Recognized colours all shades of fawn, white cream, blue, black and fawn and white pied.

Height and Weight: 32—38 cm; maximum 5 kg.

Origin of Breed: Appears to have been bred from the smallest puppies of ancient Egyptian Greyhounds. In the Renaissance period the breeding of Italian Greyhounds was influenced by the Spaniards and later by the French and English. In the nineteenth century the breeding of these miniature greyhounds was revived and they are now quite popular toy dogs.

Characteristics and Uses: Very intelligent, lively, quick, obedient and affectionate, sensitive and gentle house dog. Not so delicate as their appearance might suggest.

Saluki (Gazelle Hound)   94

Long-distance runner with its own peculiar gallop which is more like flying than running.
General Appearance: Lithe, graceful symmetrical breed giving the impression of great speed and endurance, with almost square frame and profusely feathered tail.
Head: Long and narrow, skull moderately wide between the ears, not domed, stop not pronounced. Scissors bite. Eyes dark to hazel. Ears long and mobile, hanging close to the head, covered with long silky hair.
Neck: Long, supple and well muscled.
Body: Back fairly broad, muscles slightly arched over the loin.
Legs and Feet: Muscular, forelegs straight and long from elbow to knee. Hip bones set wide apart, stifle moderately bent, hocks low to the ground. Feet of moderate length, well arched.
Tail: Long, set low and carried naturally in a curve, well feathered on underside.
Coat: Smooth, of soft silky texture, slight feather on the legs, long silky hair on ears.
Colour: All colours except pure black are acceptable.
Height and Weight: Dogs 54—71 cm, bitches rather less tall; weight proportionate to height (14—25 kg).
Origin of Breed: Descended from original breed native to North Africa and Persia.
Characteristics and Uses: Gentle and spirited appearance, as intelligent as any other breed, rather melancholy and aloof, shy with strangers but excessively devoted to its master. In the Arab world used for hunting the gazelle, elsewhere for racing. Needs patience to train.

Borzoi   122

An aristocrat among dogs.
General Appearance: A very graceful and elegant dog, harmoniously built, possessing courage, muscular power and great speed.
Head: Long and lean, skull very slightly domed and narrow, stop not perceptible. From above the skull should look narrow, tapering very gradually to the tip of the nose. Eyes dark and keen, set obliquely, placed well back but not too far apart. Ears small and fine, should be active and responsive, when alert should be erect, in repose nearly touching the occiput.
Neck: Clean, slightly arched, reasonably long, powerful.
Body: Shoulders clean, sloping well back, fine at withers. Brisket of great depth, back rising in a graceful arch from near the shoulder with a well balanced fall away. Arch more pronounced in dogs than bitches. Loins broad and very powerful with plenty of muscle. Hind quarters wider than shoulders.
Legs and Feet: Forelegs lean and straight, seen from front like narrow blades, elbows turned neither in nor out, wide at shoulder, narrowing down to the foot. Thighs long, well developed with good second thigh. Hind legs long and muscular. Stifles well bent. Long forefeet, hind feet hare-like.
Tail: Long, rather low set. Well feathered, carried low. From level of hocks may be sickle-shaped but not ringed.
Coat: Long and silky (never woolly), flat or wavy or rather curly. Short and smooth on head, ears and front legs. On neck the frill profuse and rather curly. Forelegs, chest, hind quarters and tail have profuse feathering.
Colour: Most highly prized are pure white, white with yellow, orange, red, brindle or grey markings, or any one of these colours without white.
Height and Weight: Average height of dogs 75.5 cm, bitches 71 cm; weight in proportion (35—45 kg).
Origin of Breed: Descended from sight hounds which reached European Russia with the Mongolian tribes. In Russia they were crossed with domestic breeds of herding dogs and adapted themselves to the harsh climate by growing a rich, dense coat.
Characteristics and Uses: No less clever than other breeds, self-confident, sensitive and not easy to manage. Typical racing dog. In the Soviet Union still used for hunting wolves and foxes. A sight hound. Unsuitable for small flats and houses.

Afghan Hound   116

The most decorative of all breeds of dog.

General Appearance: The whole appearance of the dog should give the impression of strength and dignity combining speed and power. An oriental expression is typical of the breed.

Head: Skull long, not too narrow with prominent occiput. Foreface long with strong jaws and slight stop. Nose preferably black but can be liver in light-coloured dogs. Eyes nearly triangular, slanting slightly upwards from the inner corner to the outer. Ears set low and well back, carried close to the head.

Neck: Long, strong with proud carriage of the head.

Body: Back level, moderate in length, well set back, well muscled, the back falling slightly away to the stern.

Legs and Feet: Shoulders long and powerful. Forelegs straight, well boned, elbows held in. Hind legs powerful, well bent. Hind feet not quite as long as forefeet, covered with long, thick hair.

Tail: Not too short, set low with ring at the end. Raised when in action, sparsely feathered.

Coat: Long and very fine on ribs, fore and hind quarters and flanks. Short on back and foreface. Hair long from forehead backward with silky topknot.

Colour: All colours are acceptable.

Height and Weight: Dogs 68.5—73.5 cm, bitches 61—68 cm; weight not officially prescribed.

Origin of Breed: Original hunting breed from Afghanistan.

Characteristics and Uses: Elegant, very striking dog, dignified and aloof but affectionate with own family. Extremely fast and hardy. Used as racing hound. Needs a great deal of exercise and coat needs considerable attention. Not easy to train.

Irish Wolfhound   125

The largest dog in the world though not so heavy as the Great Dane.

General Appearance: Rough-haired hound of great size and commanding appearance, strong but gracefully built with easy and active movements.

Head: Long, the frontal bones of the forehead very slightly raised and very little indentation between the eyes. Skull not too broad, muzzle long and moderately pointed, scissors bite. Eyes dark. Ears small and greyhound-like in carriage.

Neck: Rather long, very strong and muscular, without dewlap.

Body: Chest very deep, breast wide, back rather longer than short. Loins arched, belly well drawn up.

Legs and Feet: Shoulders muscular, forelegs strong and straight, elbows well under, turned neither inwards nor outwards. Muscular thighs and second thighs, hocks well let down, turned neither in nor out. Feet moderately large and round.

Tail: Long and slightly curved, of moderate thickness and well covered with hair.

Coat: Rough and hard on body, legs and head; especially wiry and long over eyes and under jaw.

Colour: Grey, brindle, red, black, pure white, fawn or any colour that appears in the Deerhound.

Height and Weight: Dogs at least 79 cm, bitches at least 71 cm; dogs at least 54 kg, bitches at least 41 kg.

Origin of Breed: By crossing original dogs with Deerhounds and Great Danes.

Characteristics and Uses: Quiet, self-confident, incorruptible and watchful house dog. Not encountered very often. Needs a great deal of exercise, space and feeding.

Dalmatian 76

Similar in appearance to a long-legged hound.

General Appearance: Moderately large, well balanced, muscular and active dog. Symmetrical in outline.

Head: Of fair length, the skull flat, reasonably broad between the ears, a moderate stop. Eyes medium-sized, round, set fairly far apart. Ears set rather high, of moderate size, carried close to the head. Should be spotted.

Neck: Fairly long, slightly arched, straight and tapering, free from throatiness.

Body: Chest not too wide but deep and capacious, ribs well sprung. Powerful level back, loins strong, clean and muscular, slightly arched.

Legs and Feet: Forelegs perfectly straight with strong round bone, elbows close to the body. Hind legs with clean muscles and well developed second thigh, hocks well defined. Feet round and compact.

Tail: Strong at root, gradually tapering towards the end, carried in a slightly upward curve, preferably spotted.

Coat: Short, hard and dense, sleek and glossy.

Colour: Ground colour should be pure white with round, black or liver spots which should not run together but be well defined.

Height and Weight: Dogs 55—60 cm, bitches 50—55 cm; 25—30 kg.

Origin of Breed: Believed to have come either from Italy-Spain or from India. Present standard developed in England.

Characteristics and Uses: Devoted, intelligent, quick to learn, elegant utility and guard dog. It is not true that Dalmatians are inclined to be treacherous. Originally used as a gundog and known as the Bengali Bracke. Recently attempts have been made to train it as a gundog once more. Needs plenty of exercise. Good pet and companion dog.

Chow Chow 56

A breed noted for its blueish-black tongue and unusual disposition.

General Appearance: Active, compact, short-coupled and well balanced dog, with tail carried over the back. Short- and long-haired varieties.

Head: Skull flat and broad with little stop. Muzzle moderate in length, broad from the eyes. Nose black and large. Eyes dark and small. Ears small and thick, slightly rounded at the tip, carried erect but well forward over the eyes. Tongue blueish-black. Flews and roof of mouth black.

Neck: Strong, full, slightly arched.

Body: Chest broad and deep. Back short, straight and strong. Loins powerful.

Legs and Feet: Forelegs perfectly straight, of moderate length and with good bone. Hind legs muscular and hocks well let down, perfectly straight. Feet small, round and cat-like.

Tail: Set high, carried well over the back.

Coat: Abundant, straight, dense and stand-off.

Colour: Solid black, red, blue, fawn, cream or white.

Height and Weight: Dogs minimum height 45.5 cm, bitches rather less; weight commensurate to size.

Origin of Breed: Comes from China and is probably akin to breeds of Siberian spitz.

Characteristics and Uses: Dog with strong nerves, quiet, serious, dignified, not pugnacious but utterly fearless. Extremely aloof, devoted only to its own master. Excellent companion for those who like a quiet life. Does not submit to training and hates to be teased.

Poodle   32, 44, 69

One of the oldest and most intelligent breeds of dog whose characteristic appearance comes from the trimming of the coat. Developed in France.

General Appearance: Moderately large, well balanced, elegant looking dog, carrying itself proudly, with curly or corded coat.

Head: Long and fine with slight peak at the back. Skull not too broad and with moderate stop. Foreface strong and well chiselled, not falling away under the eyes, bones and muscle flat. Lips tight fitting. Chin well defined. Whole head must be in proportion to the size of the dog. Eyes almond-shaped, dark, not too close together, full of fire and intelligence. Ears long, wide, low set, hanging close to the face.

Neck: Well proportioned, of good length. Skin fitting tightly at the throat.

Body: Chest deep and moderately wide, ribs well sprung and rounded. Back short, strong, slightly hollowed, loins broad and muscular.

Legs and Feet: Shoulders strong and muscular, sloping well to the back, forelegs set straight from the shoulders, well muscled. Thighs well developed and muscular, well bent stifles, well let down hocks, hind legs turning neither in nor out. Pasterns strong, tight feet proportionately small, oval in shape, turning neither in nor out, toes arched, pads thick and hard.

Tail: Set rather high, well carried, thick at root, docked.

Coat: Very profuse and dense, of good harsh texture without knots or tangles. All short hair close, thick and curly.

Colour: All solid colours. White and cream poodles have black nose, lips and eyerims, black toenails desirable. Brown poodles have dark amber eyes, dark liver nose. Apricot poodles have dark eyes with black points or deep amber eyes with liver points. Black, silver and blue poodles should have black nose, lips, eyerims and toenails.

Height and Weight: Standard Poodle 46—60 cm, **Miniature Poodle** 35—45 cm, **Toy Poodle** under 35 cm; weight not officially prescribed. The Miniature and Toy Poodle should be exact replicas of the Standard Poodle except for size.

Origin of Breed: One theory maintains that the Poodle's ancestors were old shaggy herding dogs, another that it is descended from an old 'water dog' used for retrieving water birds, and a third affirms that the Poodle was derived from crossing these two ancient breeds. This last is supported by the fact that the Poodle can have one of two kinds of coat: curly like that of the herding dog or corded like that of the water dog.

Characteristics and Uses: Very teachable, clever and attentive, amenable but at the same time excitable and always on the go. An excellent companion and therefore in great demand as a pet. Coat requires a great deal of care and attention.

French Bulldog 20

A breed which, at first sight, is rather like a small edition of the British Bulldog.
General Appearance: Rather small, compact, stockily built dog, with smooth coat and short, blunt muzzle.
Head: Massive, square and broad. Skull nearly flat between the ears, with a domed forehead and loose skin forming symmetrical wrinkles. Nose extremely short and wide. Eyes dark, round, neither sunken nor prominent. Bat ears of medium size.
Neck: Powerful, with loose skin at throat but not exaggerated, well arched and thick.
Body: Short, muscular and well rounded, with deep brisket and roach back, wide at shoulders and narrowing at the loins, good 'cut up' and well sprung.
Legs and Feet: Forelegs set wide apart, straight boned, strong, muscular and short. Hind legs strong and muscular, longer than forelegs. Small compact feet.
Tail: Very short, set low, either straight or kinked.
Coat: Fine, smooth, lustrous, short and close.
Colour: Brindle, pied or fawn.
Height and Weight: Height not officially prescribed; dogs 8—14 kg, bitches 7—10 kg.
Origin of Breed: According to one theory the French Bulldog is a toy version of the British Bulldog, developed in France in the late nineteenth century.
Characteristics and Uses: An unusually attractive dog, very intelligent, quiet but at the same time lively. A discreet and undemanding companion. Suitable for small urban homes.

Pug 26

English breed rather like the Mastiff in miniature.
General Appearance: A smallish, square, thickset dog of compact form and well knit proportions, with short muzzle and curly tail.
Head: Large, massive, round but not apple-headed, with no indentation of the skull. Muzzle short, blunt, square but not upturned, wrinkles large and deep. Eyes dark, very large, bold and prominent. Ears thin, small and soft — rose- or button-shaped — the latter being preferred.
Neck: Short, strong, muscular with loose skin.
Body: Short and cobby, wide in chest and well ribbed. Short muscular loins.
Legs and Feet: Moderately long, strong, set well under the body. Compact feet neither as long as hare feet nor as round as cat feet, nails black.
Tail: Known as the twist, curled as tightly as possible over the hip.
Coat: Fine, smooth, soft, short and glossy.
Colour: Silver, apricot fawn or black. The muzzle or mask, ears, moles on cheeks, thumbmark or diamond on forehead and the face as black as possible.
Height and Weight: Up to 32 cm; 7—8 kg.
Origin of Breed: Some regard it as a short-haired offshoot of the Pekingese.
Characteristics and Uses: Lively, engaging, very quick in the uptake, wary, affectionate and devoted to its owner. Not in the least pugnacious. Excellent pet and watchdog. Needs plenty of exercise if it is not to get too fat.

Typical 'man's' dog.

General Appearance: Powerfully built, robust, sinewy, nearly square dog (length of body equal to height at shoulders).

Head: Strong and elongated, gradually narrowing from the ears to the eyes and thence forward to the tip of the nose. Medium stop accentuating prominent eyebrows. Powerful muzzle, bridge of nose straight. Nose large and black. Eyes medium-sized, dark, oval. Ears set high and dropping forward to temple, in many European countries cropped to a point.

Neck: Moderately long, nape strong and slightly arched, skin close to throat.

Body: Chest moderately broad, deep, with visible strong breast bone reaching down at least to the elbow and rising backward to the loins. Back strong and straight with short, well developed loins, ribs well sprung.

Legs and Feet: Strongly muscled. Forelegs straight with strong bone. Thighs slanting and flat. Feet short, round, extremely compact with close-arched toes.

Tail: Set and carried high, cut down to three or four joints.

Coat: Hard and wiry, dense, just short enough for smartness. Bristly, stubby moustache and chin whiskers and arched bushy eyebrows.

Colour: Pure black or pepper and salt.

Height and Weight: 45—50 cm; weight proportionate (15—17 kg).

Origin of Breed: Old breed developed in Germany.

Characteristics and Uses: Quiet, teachable, gentle with own family and good-natured to children, playful but wary of strangers. An excellent pet and watchdog. Not much given to barking.

Affenpinscher (Monkey Dog)   12

Ideal dog for city life and for small flats.

General Appearance: Small but every inch a dog, tough, with round apple head. On the European continent and in America the ears are usually cropped. Tail docked short.

Head: Round but not heavy, domed and with a very prominent brow, muzzle short, undershot though the teeth cannot be seen when the mouth is closed. Nose black. Eyes round and black. Ears set high, in many countries cropped to a point.

Neck: Short and straight.

Body: Length roughly the same as height at the shoulder, brisket fairly deep, somewhat flat when viewed from the side, imperceptible transition from line of the belly to flanks.

Legs and Feet: Straight with firm shoulders. Hind legs set straight beneath the loins, hock joint not too much angled. Feet short and compact.

Tail: Set high, carried erect, docked short.

Coat: Thick and short on some parts of the body, longer and tousled on others, mostly harsh. Conspicuous eyebrows and whiskers. Face has a monkey-like expression.

Colour: Usually black but other colours are acceptable.

Height and Weight: 25—28 cm; weight not officially prescribed.

Origin of Breed: Improved from original German breed.

Characteristics and Uses: Typical house dog, affectionate, lively with quickly changing moods, extremely courageous, inclined to bark and snap. Suspicious of strangers. Needs little special attention and can live in a small space. Whelping difficulties possible, veterinary surgeon should be present.

Smooth-haired German Pinscher 54

Medium-sized, smooth-haired dog, sometimes known as Mini-Dobermann.
General Appearance: Very elegant and agile, square built, sinewy and muscular.
Head: Long and narrow with a slightly defined stop. The line of the brow and of the bridge of the nose are parallel, muzzle straight, skull flat. Eyes dark, medium-sized and oval. Ears set high and cropped on the continent of Europe and in America.
Neck: Long, slim with strongly developed nape.
Body: Squarely built, brisket deep and on the broad side, pronounced breast bone, belly slightly tucked in.
Legs and Feet: Shoulder blades sloping, forefront divided by projecting breast bone, forearms and pasterns upright. Hind legs well bent. Short cat feet.
Tail: Set high, docked to three joints, carried erect.
Coat: Short, dense, smooth, flat and glossy.
Colour: Black and tan, pure black, brown to stag red, brown, chocolate coloured or blue-grey with red or yellow markings, pepper and salt.
Height and Weight: 40—48 cm; 9—16 kg.
Origin of Breed: Original German breed.
Characteristics and Uses: Graceful, intelligent, animated, playful even in old age, teachable, wary and pugnacious, makes a good watchdog, devoted companion with a love of children. Needs a firm hand and constant contact with man.

Miniature Pinscher 16

Miniature edition of the Smooth-haired German Pinscher. One of the smallest breeds of toy dog.
General Appearance: Well balanced, sturdy, compact, elegant, short-coupled, smooth-coated toy dog.
Head: Rather more elongated than short and round, without conspicuous cheek formation. Skull flat when viewed from the front. Muzzle rather long and proportionate to the skull. Nose well formed, black with the exception of livers and blues which may have self-coloured noses. Eyes fitting well into the face, neither too full nor round, neither too little nor slanting. Ears set high, small, erect or dropped, in Europe cropped to a point.
Neck: Strong yet graceful, slightly arched.
Body: Square, back line straight, slightly sloping to the rear, belly moderately tucked up. Ribs well sprung, deep. Viewed from top slightly wedge-shaped.
Legs and Feet: Forelegs straight, shoulders clean, sloping. Hind legs well muscled, hocks turning neither in nor out. Feet cat-like.
Tail: Set high, docked short.
Coat: Smooth, hard, short, straight and lustrous.
Colour: Black, blue, chocolate with sharply defined tan markings. Solid red of various shades. Slight white on chest permissible but undesirable.
Height and Weight: 25—30 cm; weight not officially prescribed (about 4 kg).
Origin of Breed: Developed from Smooth-haired German Pinscher.
Characteristics and Uses: Very intelligent, animated, fearless, pugnacious, good ratter. Very affectionate with members of own family and energetically protects their property. Excellent pet for town-dwellers. Needs no special care.

Bichon Frisé 22

Also known as the Tenerife Pinscher.
General Appearance: Small dog with long curly coat, richly feathered tail and expressive eyes.
Head: Skull rather longer than foreface, flat, only slight stop, muzzle moderately long, not heavy, cheeks flat, lips fine, scissors bite. Nose black and shining. Eyes moderately large, rather rounded, dark. Ears pendent, well coated with hair.
Neck: Fairly long, carried proudly.
Body: Loins broad, well muscled, slightly arched, flanks tucked in at the belly, brisket well developed, rather deep, breast bone clearly visible.
Legs and Feet: Forelegs straight when viewed from the front, fine bones, thighs broad and well muscled. Black toenails are preferred but it is not easy to achieve this ideal.
Tail: Should be held high, raised at the level of the spine but not curling over. It should not touch the back though the feathers may.
Coat: Long, fine and silky, twisting into curls rather like the coat of a Mongolian goat. For show purposes the muzzle and feet are slightly stripped.
Colour: Pure white.
Height and Weight: Up to 30 cm; weight not officially prescribed (under 5 kg).
Origin of Breed: Developed in France and Belgium from dogs probably brought to these countries by the Spaniards.
Characteristics and Uses: Playful and gay, lively little lapdog which gives great pleasure to its owner.

Maltese 11

One of the smallest breeds.
General Appearance: Smart, lively and alert little dog with body longer than height at the shoulder.
Head: From stop to centre of skull and stop to tip of the nose equally balanced. Stop defined. Nose pure black. Eyes dark brown, set in centre of cheek and not bulging. Ears long and well feathered hanging close to the side of the head.
Neck: Of medium length, set on well sloped shoulders, erect.
Body: Well balanced, short and cobby, ribs well sprung, back straight from shoulders to tail, rump broad, belly tucked in.
Legs and Feet: Forelegs short and straight, shoulders well sloped. Hind legs short, nicely angulated. Feet round, pads black.
Tail: Well arched over the back and feathered.
Coat: Of good length, straight and silky, not woolly. Average length 22 cm.
Colour: Pure white, slight lemon markings should not be penalized.
Height and Weight: Dogs 21—26 cm, bitches 20—25 cm; about 3 kg.
Origin of Breed: The Maltese comes from the Mediterranean area where its ancestors were bred at the time of the Roman Empire.
Characteristics and Uses: Sweet-tempered, intelligent, faithful, suspicious of strangers. Excellent companion for those who want a dog purely for pleasure. Coat needs careful attention.

Lhasa Apso   14

A breed rather similar to a miniature sheepdog.

General Appearance: A small dog with a very long coat, drooping ears and tail carried over the back.

Head: Covered with heavy growth of hair falling over the eyes, good whiskers and beard. Skull fairly narrow, not quite flat, but not domed or apple-shaped. Foreface straight with medium stop. Nose black, can have scissors bite in reverse. Eyes dark, medium-sized, round, frontally placed. Ears pendent, heavily feathered.

Neck: Strong, covered with a dense mane, which is more pronounced in dogs than bitches.

Body: Compact. Length of back greater than height at the shoulder, well ribbed up, level topline, strong loin.

Legs and Feet: Forelegs straight, well furnished with hair. Hind legs well developed, also well coated. Feet round, cat-like, well feathered.

Tail: Set high, carried well over the back, well feathered.

Coat: Top coat heavy, straight and hard, not woolly or silky. Dense undercoat.

Colour: Golden, sandy, honey, dark grizzle, slate, smoke, particoloured, black, white or brown.

Height and Weight: Dogs 25—28 cm, bitches rather smaller; 6—7 kg.

Origin of Breed: Original Tibetan breed.

Characteristics and Uses: Gay, intelligent, teachable, assertive but chary of strangers. Originally used as a watchdog, now growing more and more popular as a pet for town-dwellers.

Shih Tzu   13

Small dog often known as Tibetan Lion Dog.

General Appearance: Very active, lively and alert with distinctly arrogant carriage.

Head: Broad and round, wide between the eyes. Muzzle square and short. Mouth level or slightly underhung. Eyes dark and large but not prominent. Ears large and drooping, set slightly below the crown of the skull. Heavily coated.

Neck: Medium length, set nicely on shoulders.

Body: Well coupled and sturdy; chest broad and deep, shoulders firm, back level.

Legs and Feet: Short and muscular, forelegs with ample bone, hind legs well muscled. Legs should be straight and look massive on account of wealth of hair. Feet firm and well padded.

Tail: Heavily plumed, curled well over the back; carried gaily, set high.

Coat: Long and dense but not curly, good undercoat. Hair falling well over the eyes and growing upward from the muzzle giving the head its characteristic chrysanthemum-like appearance.

Colour: All colours permissible but a white blaze on the forehead and white tip to the tail are highly prized.

Height and Weight: Not more than 27 cm; 4—7 kg.

Origin of Breed: Tibetan breed, possibly later crossed with the Pekingese.

Characteristics and Uses: Said to be as dignified as a Mandarin, as brave as a lion and as merry as a devil. Self-confident, tireless and bold. An ideal family pet and good watchdog. Coat needs a lot of care.

This little dog is remarkable for its smooth hairless body, with hair only on the feet and tail and the crest of the head from which it gets its name.

General Appearance: Small, active, graceful, almost hairless dog.

Head: Skull slightly rounded, moderate stop, fairly long muzzle, cheeks lean, scissors bite with prominent canines. Eyes medium-sized, moderately dark in colour, round, set rather far apart. Large upstanding ears with or without fringe.

Neck: Long, slightly arched, sloping gracefully to the shoulders.

Body: Medium-sized to long, level back, deep chest, belly moderately tucked up.

Legs and Feet: Forelegs straight, moderately fine-boned. Hocks of hind legs well let down. Hare-like feet, moderately long nails.

Tail: Carried over the back or looped, never curled. Flag on last two thirds of tail. Sparse flag acceptable, full flag preferred.

Colour: Any colour, plain or spotted.

Skin: Smooth, soft, warm.

Height and Weight: Height not officially laid down; weight around 6 kg.

Origin of Breed: It cannot be said with any certainty just where it comes from, but this breed is said to have been in existence as much as 2,000 years ago.

Characteristics and Uses: Stout-hearted, intelligent and very clean house dog which needs care in extreme heat and cold. A good watchdog even though not much given to barking.

Chihuahua   1

Two varieties are recognized: the short-coated and the long-coated Chihuahua. The world's tiniest dog.

General Appearance: Small, dainty and compact with large ears, sparkling round eyes and rather long tail.

Head: Well rounded 'apple-dome' skull, cheeks and jaws lean. Nose moderately short, black or light, slightly pointed. Definite stop. Eyes large, round but not protruding, set well apart, dark or ruby-coloured (light eyes in light colours permissible). Ears large, set at an angle of 45°, well apart, raised in excitement.

Neck: Slightly arched, medium length, slender.

Body: Level back, slightly longer than height at the shoulder. Well sprung ribs with deep brisket, rump sloping.

Legs and Feet: Straight.

Tail: Medium length, carried up over the back.

Coat: Long-coated variety: Long, of soft texture, either flat or slightly wavy, no curl. Short-coated variety: soft, smooth texture, close-lying and glossy.

Colour: Any colour or mixture of colours.

Height and Weight: 15—23 cm; 1—3.5 kg.

Origin of Breed: Short-haired variety refined from original Mexican breed, long-haired variety deliberately bred in the United States from short-haired variety.

Characteristics and Uses: Very intelligent, active, lively, teachable, wary. Typical lapdog.

Pekingese 2

One of the oldest breeds of dog, originating in China.
General Appearance: Small, well balanced, thickset dog with dense coat, having great dignity and quality.
Head: Massive, broad, flat between the ears. Eyes large and prominent, set wide apart. Ears moderately large, heart-shaped and carried close to the head. Nose very short and broad, muzzle wide, with abundant wrinkles.
Neck: Very short and thick, with strong vertebrae.
Body: Short but with broad chest, ribs well sprung, distinct waist, level back, well slung between the legs, not on top of them.
Legs and Feet: Forelegs short, thick and heavily boned. Hind legs lighter but firm and well set. Feet large and flat.
Tail: Set high, slightly curved over the back.
Coat: Long and straight with rich mane. Profuse feathering on ears, legs, thighs, tail and toes.
Colour: All colours and markings are permissible except albino or liver.
Height and Weight: 15—25 cm; 1.5—6 kg.
Origin of Breed: The breed of today is descended mainly from five specimens saved after the sacking of the Imperial Palace in Peking.
Characteristics and Uses: Intelligent, proud, dignified, energetic and courageous. Affectionate and agreeable dog suitable even for small town flats. Also makes a good watchdog. Coat requires considerable care.

Cavalier King Charles Spaniel 27

A little dog from the family of Toy Spaniels. Developed in England.
General Appearance: Graceful, well balanced, long-haired little dog with well flagged tail.
Head: Almost flat between the ears, without dome. Stop shallow. Muzzle well tapered, black nose. Lips well covering the teeth. Eyes large, dark, round but not prominent, spaced well apart. Ears long and set high with plenty of feather.
Neck: Moderate length, slightly arched.
Body: Short-coupled with well sprung ribs, back level, chest moderate.
Legs and Feet: Forelegs moderately boned and straight. Hind legs of moderate bone, well turned stifle, no tendency to cow or sickle hocks. Feet compact and well feathered.
Tail: Length should be in harmony with body, docking optional.
Coat: Long, silky and free from curl. A slight wave is permissible.
Colour: Black and Tan: Raven black with tan markings above eyes, on cheeks, inside ears, on chest and legs and underside of tail. **Ruby:** Solid rich red. **Blenheim:** Rich chestnut well broken markings on a pearly white ground. Markings should be evenly divided on head leaving room between the ears for the much valued lozenge mark (characteristic of the breed). **Tricolour:** Black and white well spaced and broken up with tan markings over the eyes, on cheeks, inside ears, inside legs and on underside of tail. Any other colour or combination of colours undesirable.
Height and Weight: Height not officially prescribed; 4.5—8.1 kg.
Origin of Breed: By crossing original breed with other spaniels, the Cocker Spaniel being one of them.
Characteristics and Uses: Very bold, lively and gay little dog with talent for hunting. Faithful family friend.

A Brief Guide to Identification of Individual Breeds

In the colour plates, individual breeds are grouped in the manner most usual at dog shows and in catalogues. In the following guide, however, they are arranged according to their size (height at the shoulder), from the smallest to the largest dogs.

In a specialist book the latter arrangement is usually avoided because of possible fluctuations in size within a standard. It has been chosen here in order to help the layman who, to begin with, will most easily recognize individual breeds by their size. When he has identified by name the dog which interests him, the reader will be able to turn to the relevant breed in the pictorial section for more detailed data.

The caption to each black-and-white photograph gives the name of the breed, the country of its origin, the height of both the dog and the bitch at the shoulder and the page number of colour illustrations.

1. Chihuahua (Long-coated);
   Mexico; 15—23 cm;
   p. 146

2. Pekingese; China; 15—25 cm;
   p. 148

3. Toy Dachshund; Germany;
   without official data;
   p. 120

4. Miniature Dachshund; Germany;
   without official data;
   p. 120

5. Smooth-haired Dachshund; Germany; without official data;
   p. 120

6. Wire-haired Dachshund; Germany;
   without official data;
   p. 120

7. Long-haired Dachshund; Germany; without official data;
p. 120

8. Yorkshire Terrier; England; without official data;
p. 118

9. Skye Terrier; Britain;
dogs 25 cm, bitches smaller;
p. 114

10. Cairn Terrier; Britain;
23—25 cm;
p. 116

11. Maltese; Italy;
dogs 21—26 cm, bitches
20—25 cm; p. 142

12. Affenpinscher; Germany;
25—28 cm;
p. 138

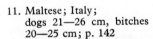

13. Shih Tzu; Tibet;
    maximum 27 cm;
    p. 144

14. Lhasa Apso; Tibet;
    dogs 25—28 cm, bitches smaller;
    p. 144

15. Scottish Terrier; Britain;
    25.5—28 cm;
    p. 112

16. Miniature Pinscher; Germany;
    25—30 cm;
    p. 140

17. Pembroke Welsh Corgi; Britain;
    25—30 cm;
    p. 46

18. Small Spitz; Germany;
    23—28 cm;
    p. 58

19. West Highland White Terrier;
Britain; about 28 cm;
p. 116

20. French Bulldog; France;
without official data;
p. 136

21. Chinese Crested Dog; China;
without official data;
p. 146

22. Bichon Frisé; France;
up to 30 cm;
p. 142

23. Sealyham Terrier; England;
up to 30 cm;
p. 112

24. Czech Terrier; Czechoslovakia;
27—34 cm;
p. 114

25. Basset Artesian Normand;
    France; 26—36 cm;
    p. 72

26. Pug; England;
    up to 32 cm;
    p. 136

27. Cavalier King Charles Spaniel;
    England; without official data;
    p. 148

28. Medium Spitz; Germany;
    28—36 cm;
    p. 58

29. Westphalian Dachsbracke;
    Germany; 30—35 cm;
    p. 76

30. Miniature Schnauzer; Germany;
    30—35 cm;
    p. 52

31. Basset Fauve de Bretagne;
    France; 32—36 cm;
    p. 72

32. Toy Poodle; France;
    under 35 cm;
    p. 134

33. Italian Greyhound; Italy;
    32—38 cm;
    p. 126

34. Shetland Sheepdog; Britain;
    35.5—36.8 cm;
    p. 44

35. Beagle; England;
    33—38 cm;
    p. 74

36. Lakeland Terrier; England;
    up to 37 cm

37. Basset Hound; America;
    up to 38 cm;
    p. 74

38. Tibetan Terrier; Tibet;
    dogs 35.5—40.5 cm, bitches
    smaller; p. 118

39. Welsh Terrier; Britain;
    dogs up to 40 cm, bitches
    smaller; p. 104

40. American Cocker Spaniel;
    North America; dogs 38—40 cm,
    bitches smaller; p. 78

41. Fox Terrier (Wire-haired);
    England; dogs 38—40 cm,
    bitches 36—38 cm; p. 102

42. German Hunt Terrier; Germany;
    up to 40 cm;
    p. 110

43. Fox Terrier (Smooth-haired);
England; dogs 38—40 cm,
bitches 36—38 cm; p. 102

44. Miniature Poodle; France;
35—45 cm;
p. 134

45. Pumi; Hungary;
35—45 cm;
p. 40

46. Bedlington Terrier; England;
dogs about 41 cm, bitches
smaller; p. 110

47. Cocker Spaniel; England;
dogs 39—41 cm, bitches 38—39
cm; p. 78

48. Great German Spitz; Germany;
40—50 cm;
p. 58

49. Basenji; Africa;
dogs about 43 cm, bitches about
40 cm; p. 70

50. Hungarian Puli; Hungary;
dogs 40—47, bitches 37—44 cm;
p. 40

51. Wolf Spitz; Germany;
45—55 cm;
p. 58

52. Irish Terrier; Ireland;
about 45 cm;
p. 106

53. Styrian Bracke; Austria;
40—50 cm;
p. 68

54. Smooth-haired German
Pinscher; Germany;
40—48 cm; p. 140

55. Whippet; England;
dogs 42—50 cm; bitches up to
44.5 cm; p. 124

56. Chow Chow; China;
dogs minimum 45.5 cm, bitches
less; p. 132

57. Boston Terrier; America;
without official data;
p. 106

58. Standard Schnauzer; Germany;
45—50 cm;
p. 138

59. Kerry Blue Terrier; Ireland;
dogs 45.5—48 cm, bitches less;
p. 108

60. Polish Lowland Sheepdog;
Poland; dogs 43—52 cm,
bitches 40—46 cm; p. 38

61. Slovak Kopov; Czechoslovakia;
dogs 45—50 cm, bitches 40—45
cm; p. 68

62. Welsh Springer Spaniel;
Britain; dogs about 48 cm,
bitches about 45 cm; p. 80

63. Bull Terrier; England;
40—55 cm;
p. 104

64. Brittany Spaniel; France;
ideal height of dogs 48—50 cm,
of bitches 47—49 cm; p. 96

65. Bavarian Gebirgsschweisshund;
Germany; dogs under 50 cm,
bitches under 45 cm; p. 82

66. Springer Spaniel; England;
50—52 cm;
p. 80

67. Wachtelhund; Germany;
dogs 45—52 cm, bitches 40—45
cm; p. 82

68. Small Münsterländer; Germany;
dogs 48—56 cm, bitches 44—
52 cm; p. 96

69. Standard Poodle; France;
46—60 cm;
p. 134

70. Samoyed; Russia;
dogs 52—55 cm, bitches from
45.5 cm; p. 66

71. Irish Water Spaniel; Ireland;
dogs 53—58 cm, bitches 51—56
cm; p. 76

72. Bulldog; England;
without official data;
p. 60

73. Old English Sheepdog; England; dogs 56 cm and over, bitches less; p. 46

74. Labrador Retriever; England; dogs 55—57 cm, bitches 54—56 cm; p. 122

75. Karelian Bear Dog; Finland; dogs 54—60 cm, bitches 48—53 cm

76. Dalmatian; Italy; dogs 55—60 cm, bitches 50—55 cm; p. 132

77. Hannover Schweisshund; Germany; dogs 50—55 cm, bitches 48—53 cm; p. 84

78. Collie (Rough-haired); England; dogs 56—61 cm, bitches 51—56 cm; p. 44

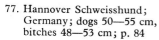

79. Collie (Smooth-haired); England;
dogs 56—61 cm, bitches 51—56
cm; p. 44

80. Golden Retriever; England;
dogs 56—61 cm, bitches 51—56
cm; p. 122

81. Airedale Terrier; England;
dogs 58.5—61 cm, bitches
56—58.5 cm; p. 108

82. Boxer, Germany;
dogs 57—63 cm, bitches 53—59
cm; p. 48

83. Hungarian Vizsla (Short-haired);
Hungary; dogs 57—64 cm,
bitches 53—60 cm; p. 90

84. Hungarian Vizsla (Wire-haired);
Hungary; dogs 57—64, bitches
53—60 cm; p. 90

85. Polish Bracke; Poland;
dogs 56—65 cm, bitches 55—60
cm; p. 92

86. Bouvier de Flandres;
France/Belgium; dogs 58—65
cm, bitches 56—65 cm; p. 42

87. Dogo Argentino; Argentine;
dogs about 60 cm,
bitches about 58 cm; p. 70

88. Pudelpointer; Germany;
dogs 58—65 cm, bitches 5o—63
cm; p. 98

89. Alsatian; Germany;
dogs 60—65 cm, bitches 55—60
cm; p. 50

90. German Short-haired Pointer;
Germany; dogs 62—64 cm,
bitches less; p. 92

91. German Wire-haired Pointer;
Germany; dogs 60—67 cm,
bitches 56—62 cm; p. 98

92. Czech Whiskers; Czechoslovakia;
dogs 60—66 cm, bitches 58—62
cm; p. 100

93. German Long-haired Retriever;
Germany; 58—68 cm;
p. 94

94. Saluki; Persia;
dogs 54—71 cm, bitches less;
p. 128

95. Irish Setter; Ireland;
dogs 61—65 cm, bitches 56—61
cm; p. 88

96. German Rough-haired Pointer;
Germany; dogs 60—66 cm,
bitches less; p. 100

97. Rottweiler; Germany;
dogs 60—68 cm, bitches 55—63
cm; p. 52

98. Dogue de Bordeaux; France;
dogs 60—68 cm, bitches 58—66
cm; p. 60

99. Briard; France;
dogs 62—68 cm, bitches 56—64
cm; p. 42

100. Weimaraner (Short-haired);
Germany; dogs 59—70 cm,
bitches 56—65 cm; p. 94

101. Weimaraner (Long-haired);
Germany; dogs 59—70 cm,
bitches 56—65 cm; p. 94

102. Giant Schnauzer; Germany;
dogs 60—70 cm, bitches 60—65
cm; p. 52

103. Hovawart; Germany;
dogs 63—70 cm, bitches 55—65
cm; p. 64

104. Sloughi; Morocco;
60—70 cm;
p. 126

105. Pointer; England;
dogs 63—68 cm, bitches 61—66
cm; p. 86

106. Kuvasz; Hungary;
dogs at least 65 cm, bitches
at least 60 cm; p. 36

107. Gordon Setter; Britain;
dogs about 66 cm; bitches
about 62 cm; p. 88

108. English Setter; England;
dogs 64—68 cm, bitches 61—65
cm; p. 86

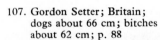

109. Bernese Mountain Dog;
Switzerland; dogs 64—70 cm,
bitches 58—66 cm; p. 32

110. Greyhound; Middle East;
66—69 cm;
p. 124

111. Bloodhound; England;
dogs about 67 cm, bitches
about 60 cm; p. 84

112. Great Swiss Mountain
Sheepdog; Switzerland; dogs
65—70 cm, bitches 60—65 cm;
p. 32

113. Polish Tatra Sheepdog;
Poland; dogs 65—70 cm,
bitches 60—65 cm; p. 36

114. Dobermann; Germany;
dogs 68—70 cm, bitches 63—66
cm; p. 50

115. Mastino Napoletano; Italy; dogs 65—75 cm, bitches 60—70 cm; p. 66

116. Afghan Hound; Afghanistan; dogs 68.5—73.5 cm, bitches 61—68 cm; p. 130

117. Newfoundland; Newfoundland; dogs 68—75 cm, bitches 62—70 cm; p. 54

118. Caucasian Sheepdog; Russia; dogs 65—80 cm, bitches at least 65 cm; p. 34

119. Pyrenean Mountain Dog; Spain; dogs 70—80 cm, bitches smaller; p. 34

120. Mastiff, England; dogs at least 76 cm, bitches at least 69 cm; p. 64

121. St. Bernard (Long-haired);
Switzerland; dogs at least
75 cm, bitches at least 70 cm;
p. 56

122. Borzoi; Russia;
dogs average 75.5 cm, bitches
71 cm; p. 128

123. Leonberger; Germany;
dogs 72—80 cm, bitches 64—74
cm; p. 54

124. Komondor; Hungary;
dogs 65—85 cm, bitches 55—70
cm; p. 38

125. Irish Wolfhound; Britain;
dogs at least 79 cm, bitches
at least 71 cm; p. 130

126. Great Dane; Germany;
dogs at least 80 cm, bitches
at least 72 cm; p. 62

Bibliography

Ashworth, L. S., *The Dell Encyclopedia of Dogs*, New York, Delacorte, 1974.

Ashworth, L. S., *The Concise Encyclopedia of Dogs*, London, Octopus, 1972.

Boorer, W. et alia, *The Love of Dogs*, London, Octopus, 1974.

Boorer, W. et alia, *The Treasury of Dogs*, London, Octopus, 1972.

Dangerfield, S., *The International Encyclopedia of Dogs*, London, Pelham, 1971.

Fiorone, F., *The Encyclopedia of Dogs*, New York, Thomas Crowell, 1973.

Fisher, C., *The Pan Book of Dogs*, London, Pan, 1958, revised 5th edition, 1976.

Leen, N., *Dogs of All Sizes*, New York, Amphoto, 1974.

McGinnis, T., *The Well Dog Book*, London/New York, Wildwood House/Random House, 1974.

Pugnetti, G., *The Great Book of Dogs*, New York, Galahad Books, A&W, 1977.

Schneck, S., *Collins A to Z of Dog Care*, London, Collins, 1975.

Summers, G., *Living with Dogs*, London, Arthur Barker, 1976.

Swedrup, I., *The Pocket Encyclopedia of Dogs In Colour*, London, Blandford Press, 1975.

Troy, S., *Dogs, Pets of Pedigree*, London, David & Charles, 1976.

White, K., *Practical Guide to Dogs*, London, Hamlyn, 1975.

Index